Kwanzaa Crafts

Gifts and Decorations for a Meaningful and Festive Celebration

Kwanzaa Crafts

Gifts and Decorations for a Meaningful and Festive Celebration

Marcia Odle McNair

Sterling Publishing Co., Inc. New York
A Sterling/Chapelle Book

Chapelle Ltd.

Owner: Jo Packham

Design/layout Editor: Linda Orton

Illustrator: Pauline Locke

Staff: Marie Barber, Ann Bear, Areta Bingham, Kass Burchett, Rebecca Christensen, Holly Fuller, Marilyn Goff, Shirley Heslop, Holly Hollingsworth, Sherry Hoppe, Shawn Hsu, Susan Jorgensen, Barbara Milburn, Karmen Quinney, Leslie Ridenour, Cindy Stoeckl.

Photography: Kevin Dilley, photographer for Hazen Photography

Photo Stylist: Leslie Liechty

Acknowledgements: A special thanks to Roberta Horton and C & T Publishing for the quilts shown in this publication.

Several projects in this book were created with outstanding and innovative products developed by the following manufacturers: DMC Corporation for floss, Deco Arts for acrylic paints, Delta Technical Coatings for acrylic paints, Plaid Enterprises, Inc. for craft supplies, Woodland Sales for glue, and Zweigart for fabrics.

Library of Congress Cataloging-in-Publication Data

McNair, Marcia Odle.
    Kwanzaa crafts : gifts and decorations for a meaningful and festive celebration / Marcia Odle McNair.
        p.   cm.
    Includes index.
    ISBN 0-8069-1777-6
    1. Kwanzaa decorations. 2. Handicraft. 3. Kwanzaa I. Title.
    TT900.K92M38 1998
    745.594'1–dc21   98-16164
                                                                CIP

10 9 8 7 6 5 4 3 2 1

A Sterling/Chapelle Book

Published by Sterling Publishing Company, Inc.
387 Park Avenue South, New York, NY 10016
© 1998 by Chapelle Ltd.
Distributed in Canada by Sterling Publishing
c/o Canadian Manda Group, One Atlantic Avenue, Suite 105
Toronto, Ontario, Canada M6K 3E7
Distributed in Great Britain and Europe by Cassell PLC
Wellington House, 125 Strand, London WC2R 0BB, England
Distributed in Australia by Capricorn Link (Australia) Pty Ltd.
P.O. Box 6651, Baulkham Hills, Business Centre, NSW 2153, Australia
Printed in China
All Rights Reserved

Sterling ISBN 0-8069-1777-6

If you have any questions or comments or would like information about any specialty products featured in this book, please contact:

Chapelle Ltd., Inc.
P.O. Box 9252
Ogden, UT 84409

Phone: (801) 621-2777
FAX: (801) 621-2788

For my children Blaise
and Leandra, through
whom I have embraced
Kwanzaa and African-
inspired information to
teach them the many
positive lessons about
our culture.

Contents

INTRODUCTION

Kwanzaa, an African-American holiday, is celebrated from December 26th through January 1st. Kwanzaa is a Swahili term that signifies "first fruits of the harvest." Kwanzaa was founded by Dr. Maulana Karenga in 1966, as a celebration of the heritage of African-Americans.

The Kwanzaa celebration gathers together families and friends to celebrate their family ties, remember their ancestors, support their community, and give thanks for the good things in life.

Homes in which Kwanzaa is celebrated are decorated with the colors red, green, and black as well as the following symbols of Kwanzaa:

Mkeka is traditionally a woven straw mat that represents reverence for tradition.

Muhindi is corn. An ear of corn for

each child in the family is placed on the mkeka to symbolize the celebration of children and continuity of the human family.

Mazao or fruits, vegetables, and nuts placed in a woven basket are the products of unified effort and the earth's abundance.

Zawadi are simple handmade Afrocentric gifts or books, which have an emphasis placed on cultural and educational values.

Kinara, the seven-branched candle holder, is symbolic of the African people and continent.

Kikombe cha umoja is the unity cup for libation, which is used to pay respect to the past, present, and future.

Mishumaa saba are the seven candles (one black, three red, and three green) that exemplify the seven principles of Kwanzaa.

Each day of Kwanzaa is started with the question **"Habari gani?"** or "What is the news?" The return answer will be the "principle" for that day. The "principles" written by Dr. Karenga have been included under each day. Following "Habari gani?", the ceremony of pouring **Tambiko** or libation to the four points of the compass, the repeating of the Libation Statement is performed:

> For the Motherland cradle of civilization.
>
> For the ancestors and their indomitable spirit.
>
> For the elders from whom we can learn much.
>
> For our youth who represent promise for tomorrow.
>
> For our people the original people.
>
> For our struggle and in remembrance of those who have struggled on our behalf.
>
> For Umoja the principle of unity which should guide us in all that we do.
>
> For the creator who provides all things great and small.

Following the Libation Statement, the kikombe cha umoja is passed to each family member and guest, who in turn takes a sip or makes a sipping gesture.

The celebration of Kwanzaa can include the wearing of African gowns, shirts, turbans, and other native attire throughout the seven days. To set the mood, home decor can consist of a Kwanzaa flag or banner; kente cloth (African cloth) as a table covering; the mkeka with muhindi and mazao; the kinara and mishumaa saba; the kikombe cha umoja; and, any other Afrocentric decorations of choice. Stories are shared about family members, African-American heroes, and African or American folk tales to exemplify daily "principles." Simple gifts and cards, preferably handmade, are given out during the days of Kwanzaa, or perhaps on a specified day, such as the sixth day when the **Karamu** or feast takes place.

The Karamu may consist of a combination of traditional African and African-American dishes. Guests on that day may be invited to bring a dish of their choice for the feast, making it a communal effort and to expand the

"African Critters"
Quilt designed by Susan Maynard Arnold
Courtesy of C & T Publishing

menu. During the seven days, many families choose to observe Kwanzaa by trying ethnic dishes from Africa, the Caribbean, Brazil, United States, or any other locale where African descendants reside or have resided.

This book contains craft projects, stories, poetry and recipes that will enhance any Kwanzaa celebration. Craft projects that are necessary for ceremony or decoration will need to be prepared in advance of the Kwanzaa holiday. Cards, bookmarks, and necklaces are a few of the crafts that may be created by children. A number of the crafts may be constructed as a group project and done in observance of the seven days and principles of Kwanzaa.

December 26th

Principle: Umoja or Unity
To strive for and maintain unity in the family, community, nation, and race.
Symbol: Mazao or basket of fruits, vegetables, and nuts
Candle: Black

Begin this day of celebration with "Habari gani?" answered with "Umoja," the principle of the day. In the evening, the black candle, which is symbolic of the richness and color of our skin, is lit and followed with a libation ceremony. Family members can discuss and share their feelings about Kwanzaa and what it represents to them along with the principle of Umoja.

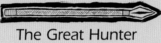

The Great Hunter
by Keith McNair

Once upon a time on the great African plains, there lived a boy named Sariti who was destined to be chief of his village. To become chief, he would have to capture the right foot of the Great Elephant. Sariti heard of hunters who had tried to capture the Great Elephant and had failed.

The night before leaving, Sariti prayed that he would be successful. He was given a spear and shield for the hunt. His father told him that other things he may need would come from within him.

Sariti traveled two miles when he saw the Great Elephant. He thought of a plan to capture the elephant so that he would be a hero when he returned to his village. Sariti dug a deep pit and covered it with straw. He planned to lure the elephant away from the watering hole and into the pit.

Sariti taunted the elephant by calling him the laziest creature on the plains. For a time, the Great Elephant ignored Sariti. He told Sariti that he was only a boy who knew nothing about greatness. The Great Elephant then charged toward Sariti in an effort to frighten him. As he moved, the elephant examined the ground and stopped before falling into the pit. Again,

he warned Sariti that he was much too smart for such trickery.

During the night, Sariti became hungry and tried to reach fruit from the high branches of the trees. The Great Elephant saw the boy struggling to get fruit and decided to help by lowering a few branches with fruit. Later that evening, Sariti became cold, but had no wood to build a fire. Again, the Great Elephant noticed the boy's dilemma and helped by pulling down branches so Sariti could build a fire.

The next morning Sariti was awakened by the sounds of lions growling several feet away. As the lions approached, a thunderous pounding of the earth could be heard as the Great Elephant charged the lions, chasing them away. Sariti was grateful for this protection and promised the Great Elephant that no harm would come to him or any elephant. He stroked the elephant's trunk to seal the promise.

Upon returning to his village, Sariti told his father that he could not harm the Great Elephant. Sariti's father knew that he had learned a valuable lesson. They declared that no hunter was to harm any elephant in their kingdom, and that kindness and compassion would always rule.

Mazao Centerpiece

Mazao Centerpiece

Materials
Wood stain
Artificial fruit, flowers, and leaves
Styrofoam form to fit inside basket
Small basket
Dried moss
Plastic spray

General Supplies & Tools
Old paintbrush
Hot-glue gun and glue sticks

Instructions
1. Lightly brush stain over fruit for antique appearance. Let dry.

2. Hot-glue Styrofoam form into basket. Arrange and hot-glue fruit, flowers, and leaves around form. Place moss in any openings and around base of form.

3. Coat contents of basket with plastic spray.

Nigerian Mango Salad

1 c. water
⅓ c. sugar
¼ c. lime juice
5 ripe mangoes, peeled and cubed
2 c. chunk pineapple
4 bananas, sliced
coconut (optional)

1. Mix water, sugar, and lime juice together in bowl. Stir until sugar is dissolved.

2. Place mangoes, pineapple, and bananas in large bowl.

3. Pour lime mixture over fruit. Cover and allow mixture to chill for one to two hours. If desired, garnish with coconut.

Golden Magnolia Wreath

Golden Magnolia Wreath

Materials
Magnolia or other leafy wreath (18″)
Gold spray paint
Ribbon, 1½″-wide (4 yds.)
Large fruit picks
Magnolia leaf picks or picks to match wreath

General Supplies & Tools
Fabric scissors
Hot-glue gun and glue sticks
Craft wire (6″)
Wire cutters

Instructions
1. Spray wreath gold. Allow paint to dry.

2. Using fabric scissors, cut 3 yds. from ribbon. Tie 3 yds. ribbon into multi-loop bow. Hot-glue remaining ribbon around wreath. Wire bow at base of wreath.

3. Using wire cutters, cut fruit and leaves from picks. Randomly hot-glue to wreath as desired.

Variations:
1. Decorate Great Harvest Wreath, using apple and grape picks, wheat, and corn.

2. Decorate Fruit and Ribbon Wreath, using apple and berry picks, and any leaf picks of your choice.

Great Harvest Wreath

Fruit and Ribbon Wreath

Fruit Wreath

Fruit Wreath

Materials
Plaster wreath
Acrylic paints: blue, med. brown, flesh, metallic gold, dk. green, med. green, purple, red, pearl white, and yellow
Med. brown antiquing medium
Crackle medium
Gloss spray varnish

General Supplies & Tools
Paint brushes
Paper towels

Instructions
1. Using paintbrush, paint wreath metallic gold. Allow paint to dry. Paint liberal amount of crackle medium over wreath, following manufacturer's instructions.

2. Using paintbrush, paint wreath in following manner: apples and cherries, red; berries, blue; plums, purple; peaches, flesh mixed with yellow; leaves, med. green and dk. green; vine, med. brown; and bow, pearl white. Allow paint to dry.

3. Spray wreath with varnish. Allow varnish to dry.

4. Paint antiquing medium onto one small section of wreath at a time, working it into recesses. Wipe excess medium off with paper towel to achieve antique-effect color. Repeat process until entire wreath has been antiqued.

Note: If a plaster wreath is not available, a wreath can be made, following Bread Dough Wreath instructions. After drying, wreath can be painted, following steps 1-4.

Bread Dough Wreath

Materials
All-purpose flour (4 c.)
Salt (1 c.)
Water (1½ c.)
Varnish

General Supplies & Tools
Large mixing bowl
Plastic wrap
Spray bottle of water
Aluminum foil
Cookie sheet
Wire rack
Paintbrush

Instructions
1. Blend flour and salt in mixing bowl. Using hands, mix water into flour mixture. Knead until smooth, roll into ball, and cover with plastic wrap.

2. Preheat oven to 300°. Pinch off two cups of dough and roll into ½" rope. Flatten rope 1½" wide. Form 8" circle on aluminum foil. Moisten ends of circle, using spray bottle, overlap slightly, and smooth surface with fingers. Cover with plastic wrap.

3. Pinch off pieces of dough and shape into fruits and leaves as desired. Keep covered with plastic wrap until ready to attach to ring.

4. Remove plastic wrap from ring, fruits, and leaves. Moisten ring, arrange fruits and rings on top as desired. Moisten wreath, place wreath and foil on cookie sheet. Bake for three hours or until completely dry. Place on wire rack to cool and leave for 3-4 days.

5. Paint wreath, then lightly paint varnish on front of wreath. Allow to dry. Repeat varnish on back of wreath.

Tunic Top

Tunic Top

Materials

Coordinating solid fabric (1-3 yds.; see Step 1)
Colorful cotton Kente cloth (2½ yds.)
Seam binding ¼" (2 yds.)
Fabric adhesive (optional)
Coordinating fabric paints (optional)

General Supplies & Tools

Fabric scissors
Measuring tape
Marking pencil
Straight pins
Coordinating thread
Sewing machine
Pinking shears (optional)
Iron/ironing board

Instructions

1. Using measuring tape, measure length from shoulder to knee of person standing straight, to determine size of tunic as shown in view #1. Multiply this measurement by two to get length for solid fabric.

2. Measure width from center of collar bone to just below elbow of person holding one arm straight out, as shown in view #2. Multiply this measurement by two to get width required for tunic. Cut solid fabric to determined width and length.

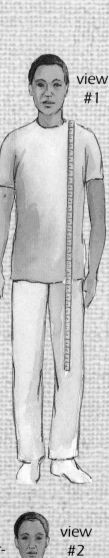

view #1

view #2

3. Using measuring tape, measure circumference of neck as shown in view #3. Divide this amount by four, then add two additional inches to get measurement for neck edge.

view #3

4. Fold solid fabric in half, with front and back sides facing each other. Fold fabric again, so right and left sides are facing each other. Mark center of the front and back with marking pencil or by cutting small triangular darts.

5. Measure and mark opening for neck edge from center fold of fabric toward sleeve area as shown in view #4. Measurement for neck equals number attained in Step 3.

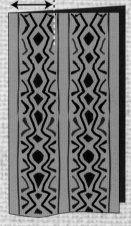

view #4

6. Lay fabric flat so front and back are not touching. Place pins in slightly oval line to mark width of 2" in center front of tunic as shown in view #5 on page 22. Continue to pin curved line, ending at shoulder edge, using the width of measurement in Step 3.

7. Machine-stitch basting stitch along pinned oval to mark line. Cut out oval for front neck edge.

8. Repeat Steps 6 and 7 for back neck edge, but mark and cut oval from center back area approximately 1" in width as shown in view #6.

9. Try tunic on at this point to make certain neck opening is wide enough.

10. Cut facing for neck edge from Kente cloth. Cut facing same shape as neck edge, using approximately ¼ yd. of fabric.

11. Place facing with wrong side of Kente cloth facing right side of solid fabric. Pin these two pieces together along front and back neck edge, making seam approximately ½" in width.

12. Place and pin strip of seam binding onto solid fabric along pinned seam to help keep neck shape as shown in view #7.

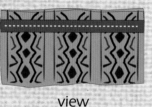

view #7

13. Baste the three pieces together, with center of seam binding attached to ½"-wide seam on fabric as shown in view #7.

14. Turn facing over so right side of facing is up. Lay tunic flat. Turn seam toward inside of neck edge and machine-stitch ⅟₁₆" seam along solid fabric neck seam.

15. Fold bottom edges of Kente cloth under and baste bottom edge of facing onto solid fabric. Machine-stitch ⅟₁₆"-wide seam over basted seam.

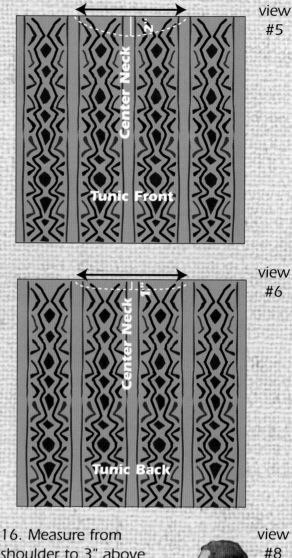

view #5

Center Neck

Tunic Front

view #6

Center Neck

Tunic Back

16. Measure from shoulder to 3" above waist as shown in view #8. Fold fabric front and back with right sides together and mark above measurement on both sides of tunic. The area below dart will be the sewn side seam.

view #8

17. Machine-stitch side seam approximately 1" in width. Start at bottom edge and stitch up to mark. Reinforce beginning and ending stitches with overlapping stitches.

18. Using pinking shears, cut edge line or sew a zigzag stitch along each seam edge to keep edges of inside seams from fraying. Using iron, press side seams open and flat and pin or baste any edges of facing onto solid fabric to keep fabrics flat.

19. Turn edge over 1" and line up with side seam to finish armhole edges. Fold this ridge ¼" under so edges do not show. Machine-stitch ¼" seam from raw folded seam.

20. Finish bottom of tunic in same manner as armhole edge.

21. Remove all pins and basted threads. Using iron, press side seams open and edge seams flat.

Variations:

1. Cut neck line into V-neck or square neck for variations. If neck edge has square corners, cut the seam binding in sections and sew binding along straight lines of neck edge. Do not place seam binding along corners of neck edge.

2. To achieve different look, cut facing from same fabric as body of tunic and iron on or glue decorative elements from Kente or patterned fabric.

3. Decorate the tunic by—
   ▪ cutting out Kente cloth in strips and highlighting certain design elements.
   ▪ using Kente cloth to face front and back of the tunic as described in original instructions.
   ▪ sewing, gluing, or ironing on fabric cutouts, using fabric adhesive.
   ▪ enhance designs, using fabric paints.

Tunic, pants, and kufi (headdress) can be sewn for younger family members, using commercial patterns.

Gelatin Jungle

Gelatin Jungle

Materials
Vanilla yogurt, 16 oz. containers (4)
Milk, 6½ c.
Envelopes unflavored gelatin (19)
Lime gelatin, 6 oz. pkg.
Vanilla yogurt, 8 oz. containers (5)
Candy (optional)

General Supplies & Tools
Saucepans, 2 qt. (2)
Paste food coloring: blue, green, orange,
    brown, black, gold
Dripper pans, 9" x 11" (2)
Disposable foil pans, 8" sq. (7)
Cardboard, 14" x 19"
Aluminum foil
Scissors
Small sharp knife
Small paintbrush

Instructions
1. Using saucepan, mix two 16 oz. containers of yogurt with two cups milk. Sprinkle three envelopes of unflavored gelatin on top of yogurt mixture. Let gelatin soften for five minutes.

2. Heat gelatin mixture over medium heat, stirring constantly until gelatin is dissolved. Remove from heat, add blue food coloring until desired color is achieved for sky.

3. Pour blue gelatin mixture into dripper pan and refrigerate until firm.

4. Repeat steps 1-3, substituting green food coloring for background color.

5. Using saucepan, mix lime gelatin with two cups boiling water. Stir two cups of cold water into lime gelatin mixture. Sprinkle three envelopes of unflavored gelatin on top of lime gelatin mixture. Let gelatin soften for five minutes.

6. Heat gelatin mixture over medium heat, stirring constantly until gelatin is dissolved.

7. Pour equal amounts of lime gelatin mixture into two foil pans and refrigerate until firm. Use lime gelatin mixture for leaves.

8. Using saucepan, mix one 8 oz. container of yogurt with ½ cup milk. Sprinkle two envelopes of unflavored gelatin on top of yogurt mixture. Let gelatin soften for five minutes.

9. Heat gelatin mixture over medium heat, stirring constantly until gelatin is dissolved. Remove from heat, add brown food coloring until desired color is achieved for tree trunks.

10. Pour brown gelatin mixture into foil pan and refrigerate until firm.

11. Repeat steps 8-10, using orange food coloring for tiger.

12. Repeat steps 8-10, using gold food coloring for giraffe.

13. Repeat steps 8-10, using black food coloring to create gray color for elephant.

14. Repeat steps 8-10, using white food coloring for zebra and bird.

15. Remove sky and background from dripper pans by turning pan upside down and running hot water over one corner of pan. Place hand under pan for gelatin to slide onto.

16. Place sky and background on cardboard covered with aluminum foil.

17. Remove and place remaining gelatin molds on cookie sheets.

18. Trace or photocopy jungle patterns on pages 26-27. Using scissors, cut out patterns.

19. Place pattern on molded gelatin and, using knife, cut around pattern. Remove cut gelatin.

20. Decorate animals, using paintbrush and food coloring. Place on background as desired. Decorate with candy if desired.

21. Keep refrigerated until ready to eat.

Gelatin Jungle Patterns
Actual size

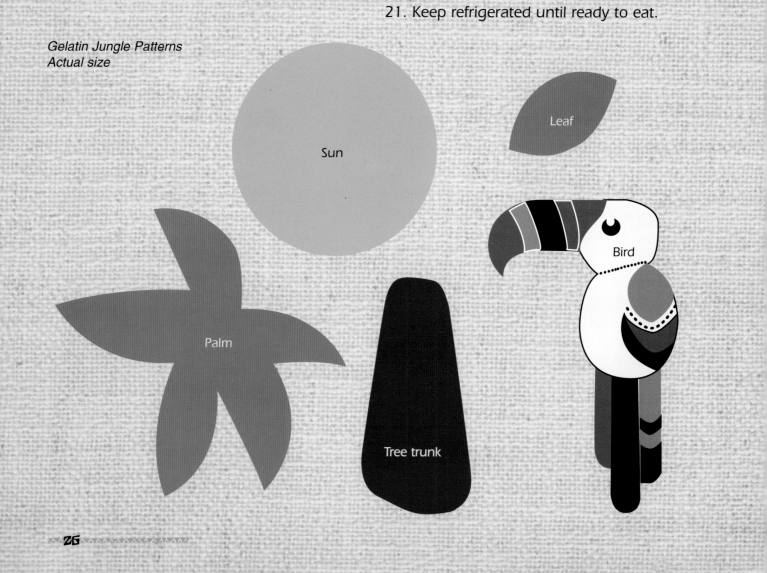

Sun

Leaf

Palm

Tree trunk

Bird

Gelatin Jungle Patterns (cont.)
Actual size

Snake

Zebra ear

Zebra

Tiger

Elephant ear

Giraffe

Elephant

28

December 27th

Principle: Kujichagulia or Self-determination
To define ourselves, name ourselves, create ourselves, and speak for ourselves instead of being defined, created for, and spoken for by others.
Symbol: Mkeka or woven mat
Candle: Red

The celebration of the individual is the essence of today. "Habari gani?" is answered with the principle of Kujichagulia. On the second night of Kwanzaa, celebration begins with the lighting of the black candle and one red candle, followed by a libation ceremony. This is the day to plan activities that define the individual.

Kujichagulia
by Keith McNair

I am a descendant of kings—a proud and prosperous race are we. The world cannot change that fact. We speak in a loud voice, that our ideas and creative abilities cannot and will not be stilled.
    The world cannot label us or detain us. Destined for continued greatness are we.

Self-determination
by Marcia O. McNair

We have one voice
Our pride is showing
We make our own decisions.

To define who we are
And to live by the right choices,
Feel power in knowing
We can name, speak, and create
    for ourselves.

Mkeka

Mkeka

Materials
Woven straw placemat
Satin ribbon: ⅛"-wide red with gold edge
   and ⅜"-wide green (6 yds. each)

General Supplies & Tools
Craft glue

Instructions
1. Beginning at top of mat, weave green ribbon down second row of mat as shown in view #1. Secure ribbon on underside of mat with glue. Weave red with gold edge ribbon in same manner, but in opposite direction of green ribbon as shown in view #1. Repeat process until three rows on each side of mat are completed.

view
#1

A straw placemat can be decorated for a mkeka as described in the above instructions; or purchase one that can be as simple as a striped basketweave or more decorative, such as a scallop weave.

K-W-A-N-Z-A-A Banner

K-W-A-N-Z-A-A Banner

Materials
Assorted fabric scraps
Black felt (34" x 7")
Fusible web
Wooden dowel (½" x 35")
Wooden knobs, 1" (2)
Black acrylic paint

General Supplies & Tools
Scissors: fabric, craft
Straight pins
Sewing machine
Coordinating thread
Iron/ironing board
Wood glue
Paintbrush

Instructions
1. Using fabric scissors, cut two 2" x 34" and two 2" x 7" strips from fabric scraps. Place strips right side down on work surface, then fold all edges in ½" and press, using iron. Fold strips in half lengthwise and press again to make bias strips.

2. Pin bias strips over edges of felt and machine-stitch in place.

3. Cut fabric scraps into five 3" x 6" pieces. Cut fusible web into five 2" x 5" pieces. Place fusible web, paper side up on wrong side of fabric pieces and fuse, following manufacturer's instructions. Trim excess fabric. Remove paper backing. Fold long edges in toward center so strip measures 1" x 5" and press. Fold strips in half and sew ends to top of banner as shown in photo on pages 32-33.

4. Photocopy or trace letter patterns on pages 34-35. Using craft scissors, cut letters out.

5. Lay assorted fabric scraps right side down on ironing board. Place fusible web, paper side up on wrong side of fabric scraps and fuse.

6. Pin letters to right side of fabric scraps as desired. Using fabric scissors, cut out letters to complete KWANZAA. Remove paper backing and arrange letters on felt, then fuse in place.

7. Paint dowel and knobs with black paint. Allow paint to dry. Slip banner onto dowel. Glue knobs onto ends of dowel.

KWANZAA Letter Patterns
Actual size

Happy Kwanzaa

Happy Kwanzaa

Materials:
7 ct. plastic canvas: Black, green, red
    (1 sheet each)
Yarn: green, red (3 oz. each)

General Supplies & Tools
Craft scissors
Yarn needle

Instructions
1. Cut green and red canvas sheets into 9¾"
x 13¾" pieces. Cut a 10¼" x 6¼" opening in
center of green canvas. Cut opening in red
canvas as shown in view #1.

2. From scraps of green canvas, cut out
letters for HAPPY, following stitching guide
on page 38. From scraps of red canvas, cut
out letters for KWANZAA, following pattern
on page 38. Cut a ¾" x 9¾" strip out of
center top of black canvas to create tabs
for hanging.

3. Place green canvas on top of black
canvas, then place red canvas on top of
green canvas. Align side and bottom edges,
then stitch canvases together with red yarn.

4. Center and stitch letters with coordinating
yarn, following stitch guide on page 38, onto
black canvas, making certain letters are
centered and evenly spaced.

view
#1

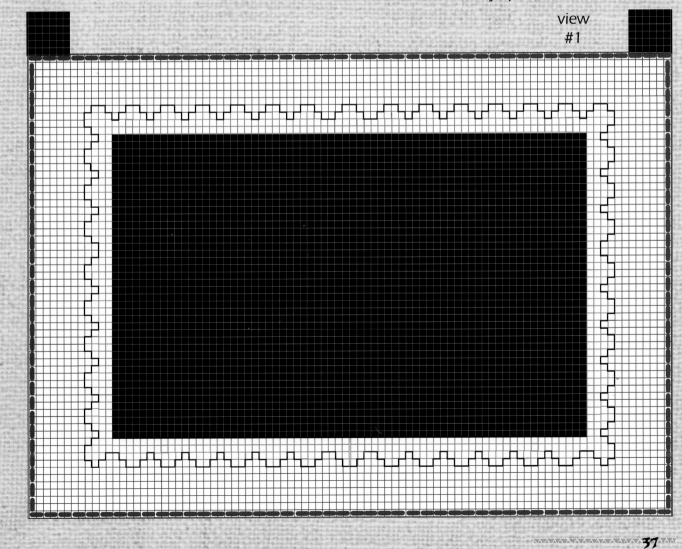

Cutting and Stitching Guide for Letters

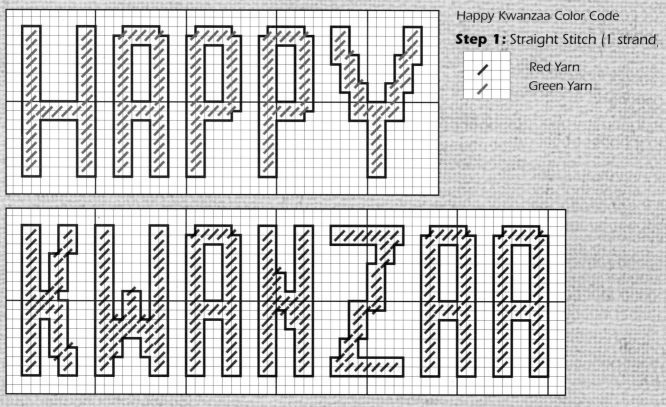

Happy Kwanzaa Color Code

Step 1: Straight Stitch (1 strand)

/   Red Yarn

/   Green Yarn

Ginger Beer

4 (11 oz.) cans powdered ginger
5 lbs. sugar
3 c. rice, uncooked
4 lemons, cut into halves
2 gal. water
Cloves, whole (optional)

1. Combine ginger, sugar, and rice in five-gallon glass container.

2. Squeeze juice from six lemon halves into ginger mixture. Add two unsqueezed lemon halves to ginger mixture.

3. Add water to ginger mixture and stir well. Cover tightly.

4. Place glass container in warm room for three to four days or until white film forms on surface. (Note: Place near furnace or heater.)

5. Strain liquid through cheese cloth into clean glass container.

6. Brew mixture by taking cup and continuously pour the liquid together until foam forms.

7. Pour into bottles and seal. Two to three cloves may be added to each bottle if desired.

8. Chill and serve.

Long-Stitch Photo Frame and Long-Stitch Tissue Box Cover

Long-stitch Photo Frame

Materials
Black 7 ct. plastic canvas (2 sheets)
Yarn: black, brown or gold, purple
   (8 oz. each)
Black felt square (8" x 10")
Black acid-free cardstock
   paper (1 sheet)
Clear acrylic frame (8" x 10")

General Supplies & Tools
Craft scissors
Black thread
Needles: sewing, yarn
Acid-free adhesive

Instructions
1. Cut out center opening four stitches larger than acrylic frame, from one piece of canvas. Using yarn needle, stitch canvas, following color code and graph.

2. Using yarn needle and black yarn, whip-stitch edges of center opening.

3. Cut remaining sheet of canvas same size as embroidered canvas. Cut felt square 1" smaller than canvas. Using sewing needle and black thread, whipstitch felt to canvas. Place stitches along second to last row.

Frame Color Code #1

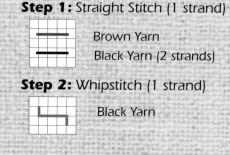

Step 1: Straight Stitch (1 strand)

Brown Yarn
Black Yarn (2 strands)

Step 2: Whipstitch (1 strand)

Black Yarn

Frame Front Panel #1

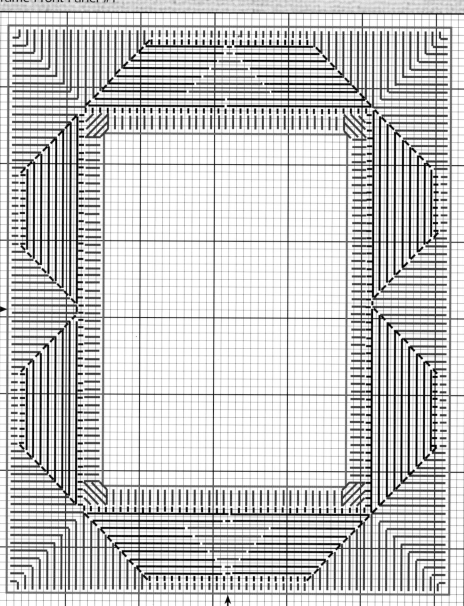

Step 1: Straight Stitch (1 strand)

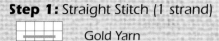

Gold Yarn
Purple Yarn (2 strands)

Step 2: Whipstitch (1 strand)

Gold Yarn

4. Place canvas sheets wrong sides together. Using yarn needle and black yarn, whipstitch top and sides of canvases together. Make four stitches in corner holes. Whipstitch the bottom of each canvas separately; do not whipstitch them together.

5. Cut cardstock paper to fit inside of frame. Center and adhere photo to paper. Slip paper into acrylic frame. Slip whipstitched frame cover over acrylic frame.

Frame Front Panel #2

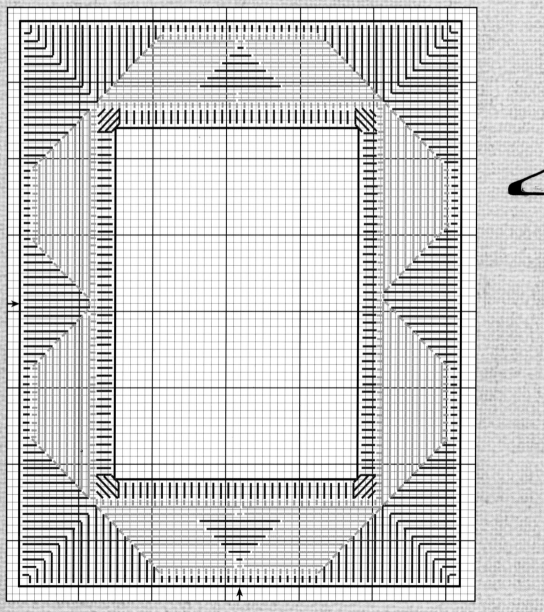

Long-stitch Tissue Box Cover

Materials
Black 7 ct. plastic canvas (4 sheets)
Yarn: Black, brown or green, black
  (8 oz. each)

General Supplies & Tools
Craft scissors
Yarn needle

Instructions
1. Cut one 5" x 10", two 3¼" x 10", and two 3¼" x 5" pieces of canvas. Using needle and yarn, stitch canvas, following color code and graphs. Cut out unstitched center of canvas.

2. Using needle and black yarn, whipstitch sides to top, then whipstitch corners together as shown on opposite page. Whipstitch bottom edges and center opening.

Tissue Box Cover End Panel #1

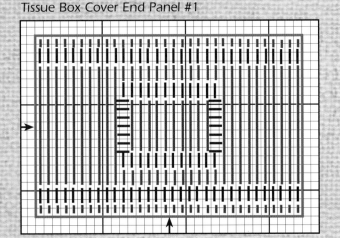

Tissue Box Cover Side Panel #1

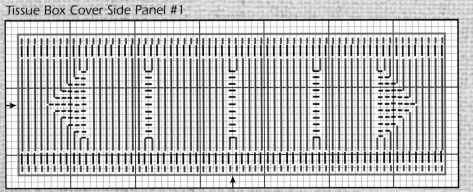

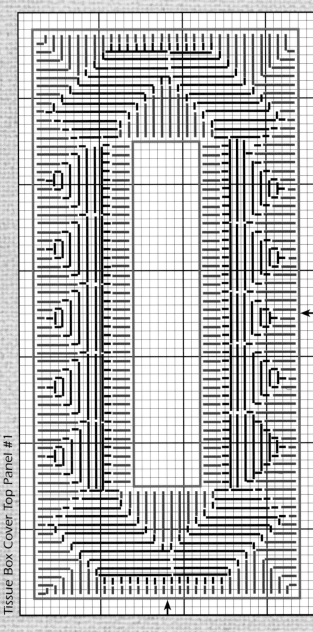

Tissue Box Cover Top Panel #1

Tissue Box Cover Color Code #1

Step 1: Straight Stitch (1 strand)

	Brown Yarn
	Black Yarn (2 strands)

Step 2: Whipstitch (1 strand)

	Black Yarn

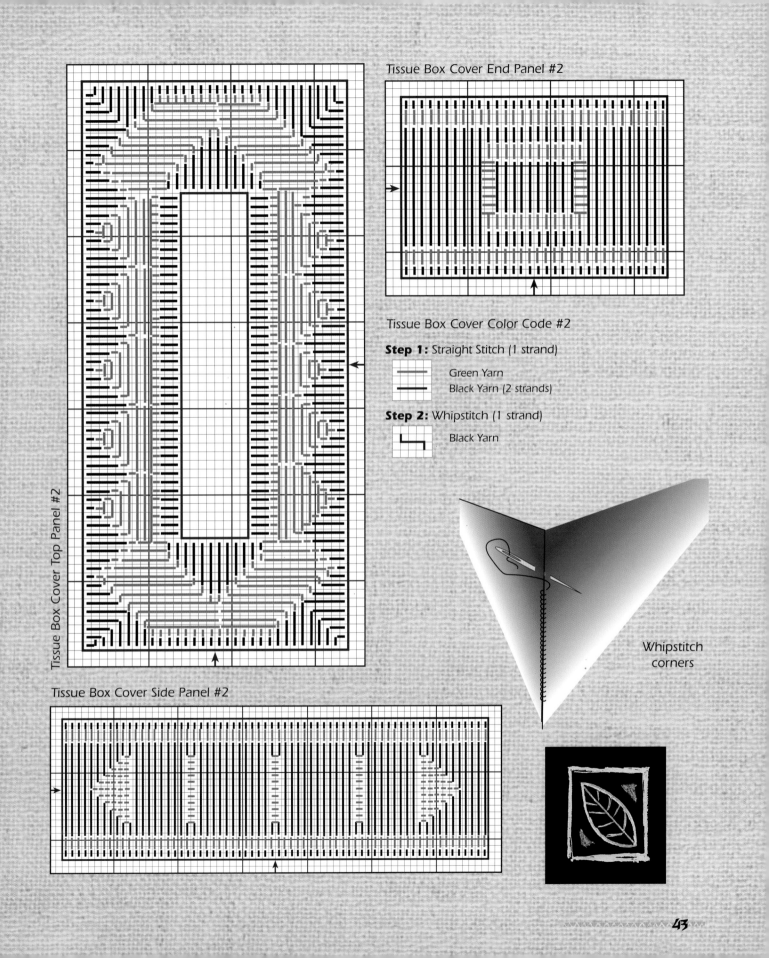

Tissue Box Cover End Panel #2

Tissue Box Cover Color Code #2

Step 1: Straight Stitch (1 strand)

Green Yarn

Black Yarn (2 strands)

Step 2: Whipstitch (1 strand)

Black Yarn

Whipstitch corners

Tissue Box Cover Top Panel #2

Tissue Box Cover Side Panel #2

Long-Stitch Eyeglass Case, Long-Stitch Bookmarks, and Magnet Bookmarks

Long-stitch Eyeglass Case

Materials

Black 7 ct. plastic canvas (1 sheet)
Yarn: black, off-white or orange, purple
 (4 oz. each)

General Supplies & Tools

Craft scissors
Yarn needle

Eyeglass Case Color Code #1

Step 1: Straight Stitch (1 strand)

╱	Orange Yarn
—	Purple Yarn

Step 2: Whipstitch (1 strand)

⌐	Purple Yarn

Eyeglass Case #1

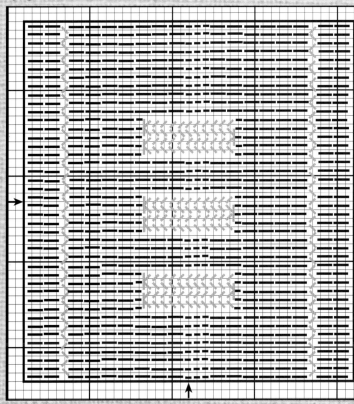

Eyeglass Case #2

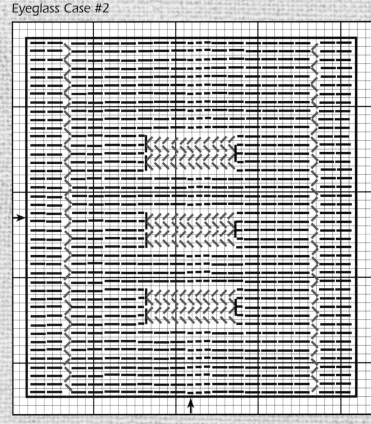

Eyeglass Case Color Code #2

Step 1: Straight Stitch (1 strand)

╱	Off-white Yarn
—	Black Yarn

Step 2: Whipstitch (1 strand)

⌐	Black Yarn

Instructions

1. Cut 6" x 6½" piece of canvas.
Using needle and yarn, stitch canvas,
following color code and graph.

2. Using needle and black yarn,
whipstitch top edge of canvas,
then whipstitch sides and bottom
together.

Long-stitch Bookmarks

Materials
Black 7 ct. plastic canvas (1 sheet)
Yarn: red, green, black

General Supplies & Tools
Yarn needle
Craft scissors
Scotch tape (optional)

Instructions
Diamond Bookmark
1. Using needle and yarn, stitch canvas following color code and graph. Using scissors, cut out embroidered canvas and 3" x 1¾" piece of canvas. (Note: Rather than having very young children use a needle, tightly wrap one end of yarn with scotch tape.)

2. Lay small piece of canvas on back of embroidered canvas and whipstitch canvases together. Whipstitch around remaining edges of embroidered canvas.

3. Cut eleven 3" lengths of black yarn to make fringe. Fold each length in half. Push a folded end of yarn through canvas hole, then slip ends through folded loop and pull to secure. Repeat process for each length of yarn.

Striped Bookmark
1. Cut out a 1½" x 6" piece of plastic canvas.

2. Using needle and yarn, stitch canvas following color code and graph. Trim ends of yarn to desired length.

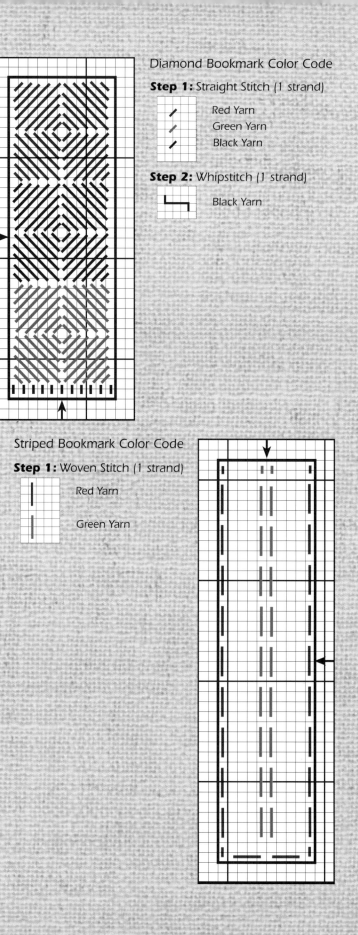

Diamond Bookmark Color Code

Step 1: Straight Stitch (1 strand)

Red Yarn
Green Yarn
Black Yarn

Step 2: Whipstitch (1 strand)

Black Yarn

Striped Bookmark Color Code

Step 1: Woven Stitch (1 strand)

Red Yarn

Green Yarn

Magnet Bookmarks

Materials:
Cardstock or Kwanzaa greeting card
Self-adhesive strip magnet (½" width)

General Supplies and Tools
Craft scissors
Ruler
Pencil
Colored markers (optional)
Rubber stamps and ink (optional)

Instructions
1. Mark and cut bookmarks 1"-1¼" x 11". Fold length of bookmark in half. If using greeting card, cut across fold, allowing for 1"-1½" width. Cardstock bookmarks can be decorated, using markers or rubber stamps and ink if desired.

2. Cut two pieces of strip magnet ¼" smaller than width of bookmark. Adhere one magnet ⅛" from bottom edge and sides of one end of bookmark. Repeat on other end of bookmark.

A bookmark can be made from scratch-board like the one shown below.

Scratchboard Bookmarks

Materials:
Tracing paper
Scratchboard
Oil pastels
Ribbon (optional)

General Supplies and Tools
Pencil
Masking tape
Chalk
Scratch knife tips: thin, wide
Tip holder
Paper towel
Masking tape
Paper hole punch (optional)

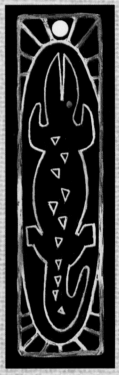

Instructions
1. Draw desired pattern onto tracing paper, using pencil. Chalk backside of pattern, using chalk.

2. Tape pattern chalkside down on scratchboard. Using pencil, transfer pattern to scratchboard by tracing over pattern. Remove tracing paper and tape.

3. Using fine scratch knife tip and holder, scratch design into surface of scratchboard. Thicken lines as desired, using wide scratch knife tip and holder.

4. Rub oil pastels as desired on white, scraped areas. Using paper towel, wipe pastel off black surface. Using craft scissors, cut out bookmark. Punch hole in top and attach ribbon, if desired.

December 28th

Principle: Ujima or Collective Work and Responsibility
To build and maintain our community together, and to make our sisters'
and brothers' problems our problems and to solve them together.
Symbol: Kinara or candle holder
Candle: Green

"Habari gani?" "Ujima," is the answer. The first green candle is lit, along with the red and black from previous days. Libation is said and the ceremony is completed. This is the day to plan a family activity that will benefit others, such as a family service project.

Ujima
by Keith McNair

The power of human touch is something we all need. As my sister and brother, I feel your joy when you are happy. I feel your pain when you are sad. Lean upon my shoulder when the problems of life seek to wear you down and, together, we shall find strength in each other.

The power of human touch is something we all need. Working side by side, we will build and maintain a community for our children. A place of refuge and harmony. Our lives are like a chain, linked through past, present, and future; and no one shall be left behind.

As sisters and brothers, we will reach out our hands and help each other hold fast to our dreams. Helping, giving, teaching, and sharing—these are the messages we bring.

Découpaged Kinara

Découpaged Kinara

Materials
Pine (2" x 15" x 4")
Decorative paper or fabric (15" square)
Découpage medium
Coordinating acrylic paint

General Supplies & Tools
Pencil
Scroll saw
Drill and ¾" bit
Craft scissors
Paintbrushes
Brayer or large dowel
Craft knife

Instructions
1. Enlarge kinara pattern 145% and copy onto pine. Using scroll saw, cut out wood. Center and drill seven ¾" deep holes in top of holder.

2. Cut paper or fabric slightly larger than side of candle holder. Brush liberal coat of découpage medium onto one side of candle holder, then gently apply paper. Roll with brayer or large dowel to smooth and remove any air bubbles. Brush découpage medium over top of paper and let dry. Using craft knife, trim excess paper from edges. Repeat process for other side, ends, and top of candle holder.

3. Paint grooves and bottom of candle holder with coordinating acrylic paint.

Kinara Pattern
Enlarge 145%

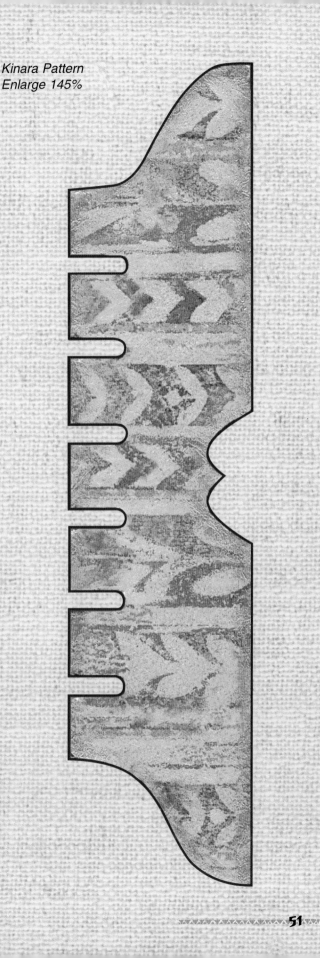

Kinara Cross-stitch

Kinara Cross-Stitch

Stitched on beige Aida 11 over 1 thread, finished design size is 8½" x 12". Fabric was cut 15" x 12".

Fabric	Design Size
Aida 14	6⅝" x 4¾"
Aida 18	5⅛" x 3⅝"
Hardanger 22	4¼" x 3"
Linen 32 over 2	5¾" x 4⅛"

Stitch Count: 93 x 66

Sweet Cinnamon Plantain

3-4 plantains, large, unpeeled,
  cut in half lengthwise
1 tsp. cinnamon
½ c. brown sugar
¼ c. butter, softened

1. Preheat oven to 350°. Using shallow baking dish, place plantain cut sides up.

2. Combine cinnamon, brown sugar, and margarine. Mix well.

3. Divide and spread butter mixture equally on top of plantain halves.

4. Bake covered plantains 35 minutes or until plantains can be easily pierced with a fork.

Anchor		DMC	

Step 1: Cross-stitch (2 strands)

Anchor	Symbol	DMC	Color
1	.		White
300		745	Yellow–lt. pale
301	– /	744	Yellow–pale
907		3821	Straw
890	O	729	Old Gold–med.
307		783	Christmas Gold
10		352	Coral–lt.
11	+	351	Coral
10	△	3712	Salmon–med.
13		347	Salmon–vy. dk.
893		224	Shell Pink–lt.
894	N	223	Shell Pink–med.
896		3721	Shell Pink–dk.
104		210	Lavender–med.
118		340	Blue Violet–med.
940	◨	3807	Cornflower Blue
872	★	3740	Antique Violet–dk.
264		472	Avocado Green–ultra lt.
266	H	471	Avocado Green–vy. lt.
267		470	Avocado Green–lt.
843		3364	Pine Green
861	⅛	3363	Pine Green–med.
862		3362	Pine Green–dk.
214		368	Pistachio Green–lt.
216	◪	367	Pistachio Green–dk.
246		319	Pistachio Green–vy. dk.
347	×	402	Mahogany–vy. lt.
324		922	Copper–lt.
349	♥	921	Copper
308	E	976	Golden Brown–med.
349		301	Mahogany–med.
1014	✳	3830	Terra Cotta
375	▽	420	Hazel Nut Brown–dk.
403	■	310	Black

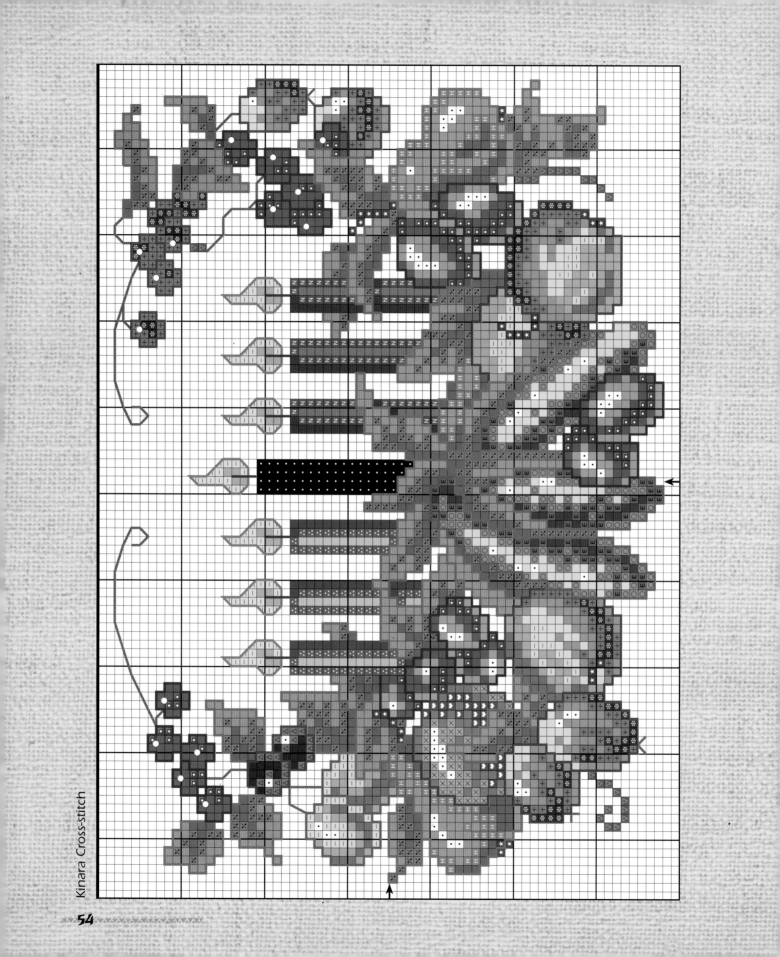

"Jambo Africa!"
Quilt designed by Joan Helm
Courtesy of C & T Publishing

Black Angel

Black Angel

Materials
Buckram, artboard, or heavy paper (9" x 14")
 for body
Ceramic angel head, ceramic hands (3")
Colorful fabrics: (20" x 30") for skirt, (9" x 14")
 for bodice, (6" x 7") for sleeve, (¼ yd.) for
 drape
Coordinating beads of choice
Coordinating beading thread of choice
Gold fabric angel wings (12")
Colorful ¾"-wide wire-edge ribbons (three
 16" lengths)
Coordinating 1"-wide wire-edge ribbon (28")

General Supplies & Tools
Fabric scissors
Glue: craft, hot-glue gun and glue sticks
 for fabric
Coordinating thread
Sewing needle

Instructions
1. Cut buckram into a triangle. Using craft glue, glue edges together to form a 9" high x 4" diameter cone.

2. Hot-glue tip of cone into ceramic head.

3. Fold skirt fabric in half, wrong sides together, to form a 10" x 30" rectangle. Using needle and thread, sew a gathering stitch along 30" raw edge. Slip fabric over cone and pull thread to gather tightly at base of head piece. Tie off gathering strings.

4. Fold bodice fabric in half, right sides together, to form a 4½" x 14" rectangle. Hot-glue or sew 14" raw edges together. Turn right side out and hot-glue or sew open end together to form a tube. Sew a gathering stitch along top of tube, ¼" from edge. Slip tube over head and pull thread to gather tightly at neck. Tie off gathering strings.

5. Cut sleeve fabric in half, forming two 3" x 7" pieces. Fold each piece in half, right sides together, to form a 1½" x 7" rectangle. Hot-glue or stitch 7" raw edges together. Turn right side out. Turn ½" of one sleeve end up into sleeve. Hot-glue hand into this end of sleeve. Repeat process for remaining sleeve. Hot-glue sleeves to back of bodice.

6. Thread beads by hand onto beading thread as desired for necklace. Tie necklace around top of bodice. Hot glue ends to back of bodice to hold in place.

7. Gather drape fabric in center, drape fabric over each shoulder. Hot-glue or stitch drape to shoulder. Drape around back of arms, gather at the waist. Secure around waist with 1" wide ribbon.

8. Paint wings with acrylic paint, allow to dry.

9. Hot-glue wings to back, making certain wings cover raw ends of sleeves and necklace.

10. Drape ¾"-wide ribbons through angel's hands. Hot-glue to secure ribbons to palms of angel's hands. Lightly curl and twist ribbon ends.

Kwanzaa Scrapbook, Kwanzaa Memories, and Family Memories

Kwanzaa Memories

Materials
Fabric (½ yd.)
Heavy cardboard, 8" x 10" (4)
Quilt batting
Optionals: embroidery floss, fabric paints,
    fabric scraps, fusible web
Ribbon (1 yd.)
Heavy-weight handmade paper (16" x 34")
Adhesive photo corners

General Supplies & Tools
Scissors: craft, fabric
Glue: clear-drying craft, clear-drying fabric
Yardstick
Marking pencil

Instructions
1. Using fabric scissors, cut four fabric panels 1" larger than each cardboard piece. Cut quilt batting into two 8" x 10" pieces.

2. Using fabric glue, adhere quilt batting to each outside cover.

3. Determine placement on fabric for front cover title. Prepare title, using desired method (embroidery, appliqué, fabric painting, etc.).

4. Center and adhere fabric panels onto cardboard pieces, folding corners inward and wrapping and gluing excess fabric to back of cardboard as shown in view #1.

view
#1

Glue and
fold fabric in

5. Mark a line across the inside center of each outside cover. Cut ribbon in half. Using craft glue, glue ribbon onto marked line, leaving equal lengths at each end to hang freely.

6. Measure and mark handmade paper as shown in view #2. Cut apart on center line to form two rows of pages. Working right to left on the first row of pages, fold the first 1" tab up, the next section down, the next section up, and so forth as shown in view #3.

7. On the second row of pages, cut off first tab. Using craft glue, adhere left tab from first row of pages to the back of first section of second row as shown in view #4 on page 61. Continue to fold sections in accordion style to form eight pages ending with 1" tab.

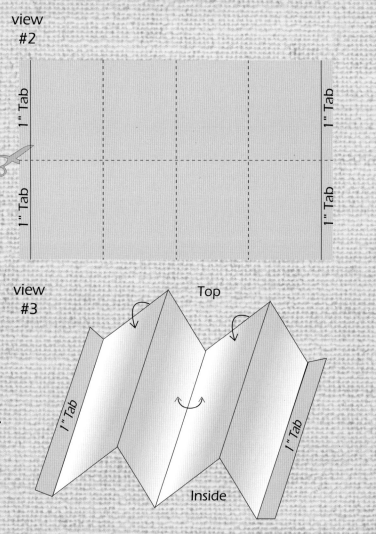

view
#2

1" Tab   1" Tab

1" Tab   1" Tab

view
#3

Top

1" Tab

1" Tab

Inside

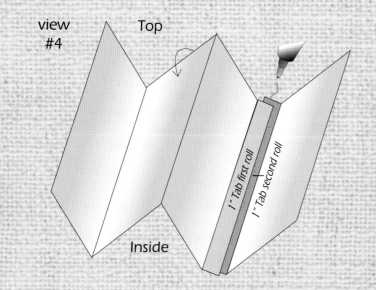

view #4

Top

1" Tab first roll

1" Tab second roll

Inside

8. Using craft glue, adhere first and last pages by their tabs to back of outside front and back covers as shown in view #5.

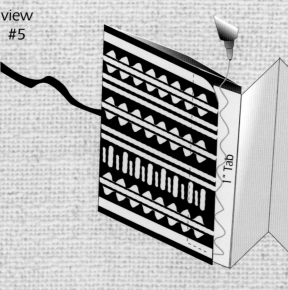

view #5

1" Tab

9. Using craft glue, adhere inside covers to front and back covers over tabbed paper sections, making certain ribbons are hanging freely on outside of covers.

10. Adhere photo corners to pages to fit favorite photos and memorabilia.

11. Tie ribbons to close book.

Family Memories

Materials
Fabric: variegated green with white polka dot (¾ yd.), green/gold/blue print (10" x 12")
Matte découpage medium
Three-ring binder (10½" x 11½" x 2")
Photo mat, 8" x 10" with 5" x 7" opening
Color copy of photograph or artwork
Gold cording: ⅛"-wide (1⅛ yds.), ¼"-wide (1⅜ yds.)
Gold tassels, 3" (2)

General Supplies & Tools
Fabric scissors
Old paintbrush
Hot-glue gun and glue sticks
Coordinating thread
Sewing needle

Instructions
1. Cut two 11" x 12" rectangles and one 25" x 13½" rectangle from variegated green fabric. Place large fabric rectangle right side down on work surface.

2. Brush a liberal coat of découpage medium onto outside front, back, and spine of binder. Place binder on center of wrong side 25" x 13½" fabric and press. Turn binder over and smooth out any air bubbles. Wrap excess fabric to inside of binder and secure with découpage medium.

3. Turn all edges under ½" on small fabric rectangles. Apply a generous coat of découpage medium to inside front and back cover. Lay fabric right side up and press in place to cover inside raw edges. Smooth out any air bubbles.

4. Apply green/gold/blue print fabric to photo mat in same manner as in Step 2.

Cut out center of mat to within ½" of edge. Wrap excess fabric to back of mat and secure with découpage medium. Center and hot-glue color copy onto mat. Hot-glue mat to front of binder cover. Hot-glue ⅛"-wide cording around edge of mat.

5. Using needle and thread, sew tassels to ends of ¼"-wide cording. Wrap cording around left side of binder. Tie a bow about 1½" from top of binder. Hot-glue bow to binder.

Kwanzaa Scrapbook

Materials
Fabric: black/tan print (2/3 yd.), copper (12" x 5"), black/tan/ivory assorted scraps (7)
Three-ring binder (14" x 10" x 1")
Ribbons: 1"-wide ivory/black print (¼ yd.), 1½"-wide ivory chiffon (¼ yd.), 2"-wide black grosgrain (¼ yd.)
Mat board (10" x 3 ¾")
Fusible web (14" x 3")
Black cording: ⅛"-wide (1 yd.)

General Supplies & Tools

Scissors: fabric, craft
Hot-glue gun and glue sticks
Craft glue
Iron/ironing board
Pencil

Instructions

1. Using fabric scissors, cut two 15" x 11" rectangles and a 31" x 12" rectangle from black/tan print fabric. Place large fabric rectangle right side down on work surface. Open binder and place cover side down in center of fabric. Wrap fabric to inside of binder and hot-glue to binder to secure.

2. Layer ribbons by centering one on top of next as shown in photo on page 59. Place on front cover, about ¾" from left edge. Fold ribbon ends to inside of cover and hot-glue in place.

3. Turn all edges under ½" on small fabric rectangles. With right side up, hot-glue a fabric rectangle to inside front and back cover to cover raw edges.

4. Place copper fabric right side down on work surface. Place mat board in center of fabric. Wrap excess fabric to back of board and hot-glue in place.

5. Photocopy and reduce letter patterns 50% on pages 34-35. Using craft scissors, cut letters out.

6. Lay assorted fabric scraps right side down on ironing board. Place fusible web, paper side up onto wrong side of fabric scraps and fuse, following manufacturer's instructions.

7. Pin letters to right side of fabric scraps as desired. Using fabric scissors, cut out letters to complete KWANZAA. Remove paper backing and arrange letters on copper fabric, fuse in place.

8. Using craft glue, adhere mat board to front of binder. Glue cording around edge of mat board.

Tips for Making Archival Scrapbooks:

◆ Purchase acid-free papers, adhesives, pens, and stickers.

◆ Use permanent-pigment inks when writing or drawing in scrapbooks to avoid fading over the years.

◆ Use pH-testing pen to test for acid in papers. Make mark on back of paper. If it is acid-free, the mark will remain blue. If there is some acid content in paper, the mark will turn green. If the acid content is high, the mark will turn yellow.

◆ When desiring to include memorabilia that has acid content, take one of the following precautions:

    1. Photocopy on acid-free paper and place photocopy in scrapbook.

    2. Spray memorabilia, using a special buffering spray (available from craft stores) that will neutralize acid and provide a protective coating to stop acid recurrence.

◆ Do not use self-stick pages to store photos. The adhesives contain chemicals that will fade, yellow, and cause photographs to become brittle.

◆ Always use removable adhesives or photo corners to attach photos and memorabilia. When it is necessary to remove photos, they will not be damaged.

December 29th

Principle: Ujamaa or Cooperative Economics
To build and maintain our own stores, shops, and other businesses and to profit from them together.
Symbol: Muhindi or corn
Candle: Red

"Ujamaa" is today's answer to "Habari gani?" The candles are lit and the libation ceremony sets the stage for tonight's celebration. As we support our local economy, we all profit together. Family members can contribute financially toward the purchase of a household item that would benefit all.

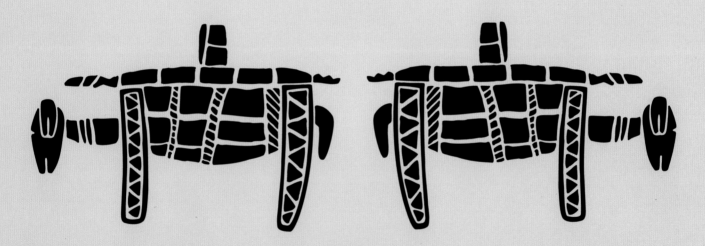

Ujamaa
by Marcia O. McNair

The marketplace
is where we exchange
goods and services with each other.

By supporting
our own,
Our businesses have grown ·
in cooperation with our sisters and brothers.

Jungle Platter and Festive Kwanzaa Cookies

Jungle Platter

Materials
Red and green plaid tissue paper
Artwork of choice
Black cardstock (1 sheet)
Green wooden plate (13")
Découpage medium
Yellow paper (1 sheet)
Black and white checkered sticker strip

General Supplies & Tools
Craft scissors
Pencil
Flat paintbrush (1")
Star paper punch

Instructions
1. Cut tissue paper into 1" squares, following tissue paper plaid pattern. Set aside.

2. Cut artwork into a 7" circle. (Make a color photocopy of artwork if it cannot be cut.) Cut cardstock into a 7⅛" circle.

3. Place cardstock in center of plate. Using pencil, trace around cardstock and remove.

4. Refer to General Instructions for Découpage Techniques on pages 122-123. Brush découpage medium to 3" section on rim of plate. Adhere tissue paper squares to rim as shown in photo on page 66. Gently smooth to release any air bubbles. Repeat process around center, penciled circle.

5. Découpage cardstock circle to center of plate. Center and découpage artwork to cardstock.

6. Punch paper stars from yellow paper and découpage to plate, referring to photo on page 66 for placement.

7. Adhere black-and-white sticker strip around rim of plate.

8. Apply three coats of découpage medium to entire plate, allowing découpage to dry between coats.

Festive Kwanzaa Cookies

Materials
Non-stick cooking spray
Ready-made sugar cookie dough
All-purpose flour
Decorator Icing (variety of colors)
Candy (optional)
Candy clay (optional)

General Supplies & Tools
Oven
Cookie sheet
Large Mixing bowl
Rolling pin
Geometric-shaped cookie cutters
Decorator bag and tips (optional)

Instructions
1. Preheat oven to 350° and lightly spray a cookie sheet with non-stick cooking spray.

2. Place chunks of cookie dough and a handful of flour in a large mixing bowl. Mix together until cookie dough does not stick to your hands. Divide the cookie dough into fist-sized balls and set aside in a bowl.

3. Lightly flour a rolling surface. Roll one ball to a 1⁄16" thickness. Using cookie cutters, press geometric shapes into rolled dough. Place them on cookie sheet.

4. Bake cookies approximately 12 minutes until lightly browned. Let cool.

5. Decorate as desired with icing, cake decorating supplies, candy clay, and candy.

Sugar Cookies

1 c. margarine, softened
1½ c. sugar
2 eggs
1½ tsp. vanilla extract
4 c. all-purpose flour
1 tsp. baking soda
1 tsp. salt

1. Preheat oven to 375°.

2. Cream margarine and sugar in large bowl. Beat until light and fluffy.

3. Add egg and vanilla, mix well.

4. Combine dry ingredients and add to creamed mixture. Mix well.

5. Divide dough into fourths. Flour surface and roll out one portion of dough to ¼" thickness.

6. Cut out dough with cookie cutters and place 2" apart on ungreased cookie sheet. Bake for 8-10 minutes or until light brown. Cool on racks.

7. Repeat with remaining portions of dough.

Buttercream Decorator Icing

½ c. butter or margarine, softened
½ c. shortening
1 tsp. vanilla, lemon or orange extract
4 c. confectioners sugar
¼ tsp. salt
2-3 tbsp. milk
Food coloring

1. Cream butter and shortening together.

2. Beat extract, confectioners sugar, and salt into butter mixture adding milk as needed until icing is light and fluffy.

3. Add food coloring and mix until color is uniform. (Note: Divide icing into smaller portions and color separately in a variety of colors.)

Candy Clay

⅓ c. margarine, melted
⅓ c. light corn syrup
1 tsp. vanilla
½ tsp. salt
1 lb. confectioners' sugar
Paste food coloring

1. Blend margarine, corn syrup, vanilla, and salt together.

2. Mix in sugar and knead until smooth, adding more sugar if mixture is too sticky. Candy clay should be pliable.

3. Divide clay into portions, according to the number of desired colors.

4. Knead color into clay until desired color is achieved.

5. Roll out clay flat and cut or hand-mold into geometric shapes. Place on cookies for decoration. (Note: Candy clay can be stored in plastic bags and refrigerated for up to two weeks.)

Harvest Tray

Harvest Tray

Materials
Wooden tray (15" x 20")
Green ceramic tiles, 4" squares (12)
Tan tile grout
Enamel surface cleaner and conditioner
Stencil blanks, 4" squares (4)
Stencil adhesive
Enamel paints: black, brown, green, dk.
    green, mulberry, orange, lt. orange,
    dk. purple, red, white, yellow
Acrylic paints: dk. green, lt. green, off-white,
    purple, red, yellow
Matte spray varnish

General Supplies & Tools
Ruler
Pencil
Craft glue
Permanent marker
5" x 7" sheet of glass, as from picture frame
Craft knife
Masking tape
Stencil brush
Paintbrushes
Waxed paper
Small checked stencil

Instructions
1. Measure and mark placement for tiles inside of tray so tiles are evenly spaced between each other and from edges of tray.

2. Cover back of tiles with glue and adhere to inside of tray.

3. Following manufacturer's instructions, prepare, apply, and clean tile grout around tiles.

4. Clean and condition tiles with enamel surface cleaner.

5. Using a permanent marker, trace stencil patterns from page 72 onto stencil blanks. Tape stencil blank to glass to hold in place. Using craft knife, cut out stencil.

6. Tape over leaves, stems, and whole grapes to prevent paint from getting in these areas.

7. Spray back of stencil with stencil adhesive. (Note: This prevents paint from leaking under stencil.) Allow stencil adhesive to dry.

8. Stencil designs onto tiles. Load stencil brush with designated enamel paint and pounce brush up and down in the stencil opening. While paint is still wet, pounce on shade and highlight colors. Stencil apples and cherries, using red paint, red and black paint for shading, and lt. orange paint for highlighting. Stencil pears, using yellow paint, green paint for shading, and orange paint for highlighting. Stencil green apples, using green paint; red paint for shading; and orange paint for highlighting. Stencil partial grapes, using dk. purple. Allow fruit portion of stenciled pattern to dry.

9. Remove tape from stencils. Replace stencil on tile and carefully stencil whole grapes, leaves, and stems. Stencil leaves, using dk. green paint, black and white paint for shading, and green paint for highlighting. Stencil stems, using brown paint. Stencil whole grapes, using mulberry. Allow paint to dry.

10. Using checked stencil, stencil checks in 1½" sections on edge of tray and tiles with off-white acrylic paint as shown in photograph on page 70.

11. Paint lines, dots, and zigzags with lt. green, off-white, purple, red, and yellow

acrylic paint as shown in photograph on page 70.

12. Paint remaining wood portion of tray dk. green. Allow paint to dry.

Harvest Tray Stencil Patterns and Painting Guides
Actual size

13. Cover tile area with waxed paper and spray tray with varnish. Allow paint on tiles to cure six days before washing.

Kwanzaa Medallions

Kwanzaa Medallions

Materials
Wood, ¼" thick pine
Acrylic paints
Spray sealer
Cording

General Supplies & Tools
Scroll saw
Medium-grit sandpaper
Pencil
Paintbrushes
Drill with drill bits

Kwanzaa Medallions Paint Guide

Instructions
1. Using scroll saw, cut wood into desired size and shape for medallion. Sand edges to smooth.

2. Using medallion paint guide, draw desired design on medallion. Paint design in desired colors. Allow paint to dry.

3. Spray medallion with sealer.

4. Drill hole large enough for cord to pass through. Thread cord through medallion, then knot.

Count the Days of Kwanzaa

Count the Days of Kwanzaa

Materials
Papier Maché Boxes: 7" x 7" x 3" (1); 4" x 4"
   x 2¼" (4); 4½" x 3 ½" x 2¼" (2); octagon,
   4½" x 3½" x 2¼" (1)
Acrylic paints: dk. burgundy, metallic gold,
   dk. green, mustard yellow
Satin varnish
Assorted miniature fruit (8)
Berries with leaves
Amber seed beads (14)
Assorted decorative beads for knobs (7)
Metallic gold and red ribbon, ⅜" wide (2 yds.)
Metallic gold number stickers (1-7)

General Supplies and Tools
Paintbrushes: flat, stiff round
Craft knife
Hot-glue gun and glue sticks
Sewing needle
Off-white carpet thread
Fabric scissors

Instructions
1. Using flat paintbrush, paint inside and outside of square box bases with dk. green paint. Paint inside and outside of octagon base with mustard yellow paint. Paint octagon and small box lids inside and out with dk. burgundy paint. Paint large box lid with mustard yellow paint.

2. Paint inside and outside of box bases and lids with two coats of varnish. Allow varnish to dry between coats.

3. Using craft knife, cut two corners on each box lid, except for large square lid and octagon lid, to form hinge and miter bottom edge as shown in view #1.

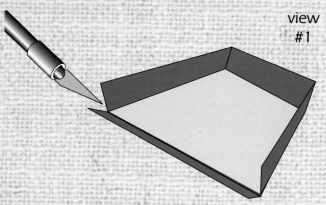

view #1

4. Hot-glue cut side of lid to corresponding box base to make hinge. Hot-glue large lid to large base.

5. Hot-glue four small square boxes on top of large box lid as shown in photo on page 75, with hinged side of lid down. Hot-glue two remaining hinged boxes on top of four small boxes with hinged side of lid down. Hot-glue octagon box on top.

6. Fill stiff round brush with gold metallic paint. Dab onto paper towel until most of the paint is gone. Dry-brush fruit by brushing paintbrush over fruit. Allow paint to dry.

7. Using needle and thread, doubled and knotted, push needle where knob is desired from outside of box lid to inside. Thread one seed bead over needle, push needle back through to the outside. Thread decorative bead and seed bead onto needle. Push needle and thread back through decorative bead and through to inside of lid as shown in view #2.

Wrap thread around thread between inside of box lid and seed bead, knot to secure. Repeat on each box lid.

view #2

8. Using fabric scissors, cut ribbon into seven 10" lengths. Tie small bow, leaving 4" tails. Tie knots in tails. Hot-glue fruits, berries, and bows as desired for embellishment.

9. Place sticker number 1 on side of octagon base and numbers 2-7 on small box lids.

Note: Place a small gift or trinket inside of each box. Box #1 is opened on the first day of Kwanzaa. A new box is opened each day.

Bead Napkin Ring

Materials
Round beads, 1" (5)
Flat faceted beads (5)
Gold-tone wire, .021 gauge

General Supplies & Tools
Wire cutters

Instructions
1. Thread beads onto wire, alternating round bead with flat bead. Pull wire and beads into circle to form napkin ring.

2. Randomly wrap wire around and between beads as desired. Secure and clip wire ends.

Crystal Napkin Ring

Materials
Assorted clear crystals
Gold-tone napkin ring
Gold-tone wire, 021 gauge

General Supplies & Tools
Wire cutters

Instructions
1. Place crystals on wire and wrap wire around to secure as desired. Continue adding and wrapping crystals as desired, leaving wire tails.

2. Secure crystals to napkin ring by wrapping tails around napkin ring and twisting wires together on inside. Clip wire ends.

December 30th

Principle: Nia or Purpose
To make our collective vocation the building and developing of our community in order to restore our people to their traditional greatness.
Symbol: Zawadi or handmade gifts
Candle: Green

"Habari gani?" is answered with today's principle. A second green candle is lit, along with the candles from the four previous Kwanzaa evenings. The libation ceremony is performed and the kikombe cha umoja is passed to family members and friends. This is a time that could be spent discussing and reflecting on the future as well as the present.

Greatness	Nia
by Keith McNair	by Marcia O. McNair

Greatness cannot be bought, it is a reward
   for word and deed.

Greatness cannot be taken away, for it is part
   of the soul.

Greatness, like the power of the sun, shall
   always shine down upon us.
Through words and deeds, we will achieve
   the greatness that is meant to be.

Greatness is my birthright,
It cannot be taken away.

My ancestors have shown the original light
That lives in my heart today.

Kwanzaa Notecards

Kwanzaa Notecards

Materials
Colored and decorative handmade papers
Blank notecards
Rubber stamps, as desired
Clear embossing ink pad
Embossing powder

General Supplies & Tools
Craft scissors
Craft glue
Embossing heat tool

Instructions
1. Cut colored and decorative handmade papers into desired geometric shapes. Glue paper shapes onto notecards in desired patterns.

2. Refer to General Instructions for Rubber Stamping Techniques on pages 124-125. Ink rubber stamp and stamp onto notecards as desired. Emboss with embossing powder.

Variations:
Create personal 3" x 5" recipe cards, using above notecard techniques, and share your favorite Kwanzaa recipe with friends.

The gift bags on pages 82-83 can be filled with goodies as well as gifts. Banana bread with an attached recipe or personal note would be a well-received treat.

Banana Bread

2 eggs
4 tbsp. butter, melted
½ c. brown sugar, light
2 bananas, ripe, mashed
1½ c. all-purpose flour
1½ tsp. baking powder
½ tsp. salt
1½ tsp. cinnamon
1 c. walnuts, chopped (optional)
½ c. raisins

1. Preheat oven to 375°. Grease 9" x 5" x 3" loaf pan. Line bottom of pan with wax paper cut to size.

2. Beat eggs in large bowl. Add butter, brown sugar, and bananas. Mix well.

3. In second bowl, combine dry ingredients. Add dry mixture to banana mixture. Mix well.

4. Pour into loaf pan and bake 30 minutes at 375°. Turn oven to 350° and continue baking for 30 minutes, or until knife inserted into center comes out clean. Cool and remove from loaf pan.

Stamped Gift Bags and Cards

Stamped Gift Bags and Cards

Materials
Colorful coordinating cardstock papers
Colorful totes and paper bags
Rubber stamps: small alphabet, gift box,
    "let's celebrate," "Happy Kwanzaa," apple,
    grape bunch, large swirl, zebra print,
    giraffe print
Colorful coordinating ribbon: $\frac{1}{16}$"-wide,
    $\frac{1}{8}$"-wide (12" each)
Embossing pens or embossing ink pad
Embossing powders: clear, metallic gold
3-d adhesive sponges
Colorful pigment inks

General Supplies & Tools
Craft scissors
Decorative paper edgers
Rubber cement
Embossing heat tool
Paper punch
Stapler

Instructions
Layered Shapes Gift Bags
1. Cut papers into varying geometric shapes
and sizes. Trim edges with paper edgers. Cut
decorative shapes from paper. Using rubber
cement, glue decorative shapes to tote bag.
Layer and glue geometric papers together,
then adhere to front of tote bags.

2. Refer to General Instructions for Rubber
Stamping Techniques on pages 124-125.
Color desired stamps with embossing pens
and stamp onto papers on front of bags. Ink
stamps with pigment inks and stamp onto
bags as desired. Emboss with embossing
powder.

3. Fold top of bag as shown in view #1.
Staple to secure <u>after</u> gift has been placed
in bag.

3-d Shapes Gift Totes
1. Refer to General Instructions for Rubber
Stamping Techniques on pages 124-125.
Stamp and emboss several designs onto
separate sheet of paper and cut out. Glue
cutouts to another piece of paper, then trim
edges with paper edgers. Attach designs to
3-d sponges and adhere to front of tote bag.

2. Color desired stamps with embossing
pens and stamp onto papers on front of
totes. Ink desired stamps with pigment inks
and stamp onto bags as desired. Emboss
with embossing powder.

Gift Tags and Cards
1. Fold paper into desired sizes. Repeat
cutting and stamping process used for gift
bags and totes.

2. Punch hole in top of gift tag and in top
of paper bag. Thread three strands of ribbon
through holes and tie into a bow.

view #1

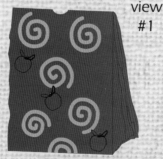
1. Gift bag

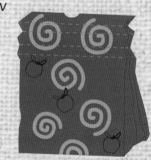
2. Accordian fold 3 or 4 times

3. Crease in middle

4. Fold up

Kente Cloth Bear

Kente Cloth Bear

Materials

Kente or African motif fabric (⅜ yd.)
Coordinating felt scrap
Polyester stuffing
Buttons: ¼" wide, round, black (2);
 ⅞" wide, flat, coordinating color (4)
Bear nose
Coordinating ribbon, ⅝" wide (20")
Decorative beads (3)
Potpourri (optional)

General Supplies & Tools

Fabric scissors
Sewing machine
Wooden spoon or chopsticks
Coordinating threads: sewing, carpet/
 buttonhole
Needles: sewing; long (7"-12")
Pins: straight, T-pins
Hot-glue gun and glue sticks
Black embroidery floss

Instructions

1. Enlarge patterns on page 88 to 200% and photocopy. Using straight pins, pin paw pad and ear patterns to felt and cut two of each. Place and pin remaining patterns to Kente fabric. Cut out pattern pieces.

2. Machine-stitch darts together. With right sides of head together, machine-stitch ⅛" seam as shown in view #1.

view
 #1

3. Using sewing needle and thread, baste gusset piece to top of both sides of head with as shown in view #2, leaving neck open. Machine-stitch ⅛" seam to secure. Turn head right side out.

view
#2

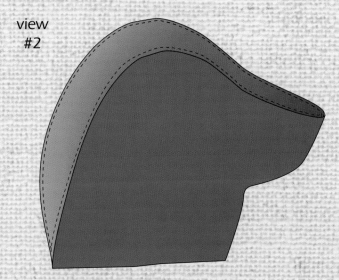

4. With right sides of ears together, machine-stitch the curved part as shown in view #3 with ⅛" seam. Turn ears right side out. Turn ⅛" raw edge of ear inside. Using needle and thread, close bottom of ear with ladder stitch as shown in view #4.

view
 #3

view
 #4

5. Stuff head, beginning at snout, with small pieces of polyester stuffing. Shape head with hand while stuffing. Push stuffing into snout, using handle of wooden spoon until firm. Continue stuffing bear head until firm.

6. Machine-stitch body darts together. With right sides of body together, machine-stitch body together with ⅛" seam, leaving opening in back for stuffing. Turn fabric right side out.

7. Stuff body with small pieces of polyester stuffing until firm. Close body opening, using ladder stitch. (Note: Body can be stuffed with potpourri mix.)

8. With right sides together machine-stitch inside arm to paw pad with ⅛" seam. Repeat for other arm.

9. With right sides together, machine-stitch inside arm and outside arm together with ⅛" seam, leaving opening for stuffing. Repeat for other arm. Turn arms right side out.

10. Using handle of wooden spoon, stuff arms with small pieces of polyester stuffing until firm. Using sewing needle and thread, close arm openings with ladder stitch.

11. Fold right sides together. Machine-stitch leg with ⅛" seam, leaving openings for stuffing and foot pad. Repeat for other leg.

12. Using straight pins, pin foot pad to leg. Baste around edge of pad with needle and thread. Machine-stitch ⅛" seam to secure. Repeat for other leg. Turn legs right side out.

13. Using handle of wooden spoon, stuff legs with small pieces of polyester stuffing until firm. Using sewing needle and thread, close leg openings with ladder stitch.

14. Using sewing needle and thread, sew gathering stitch ⅛" from raw edge of fabric around neck opening. Gather neck edge, leaving 1"-1½" opening and knot to secure. Using T-pins, pin head to body. Secure head to body with ladder stitch. Remove pins.

15. Mark eye placement with T-pins, referring to head pattern. Cut two 18" lengths of carpet thread. Double one piece of carpet thread, thread through loop of round black button. Center thread and tie knot. Using long needle, thread four pieces of thread. Insert threaded needle where eye is to be placed. Push needle through stuffing and out through back of bear's neck at seam. Pull threads tight and knot to secure. Using long needle, pull remaining ends into body. Repeat with other eye.

16. Using T-pins, pin ears in place. Secure ears to head with ladder stitch. Remove pins. Knot off thread and pull ends into head.

17. Hot-glue nose into place. (Note: Nose may be satin-stitched with embroidery floss.)

18. Cut 28" piece of carpet thread. Thread long needle with doubled carpet thread. Knot thread and stitch into opposite side of body where arm will be attached. Stitch through leg and one side of ⅞" flat button as

shown in view #5. Stitch back through other side of button, through the body, through

view
#5

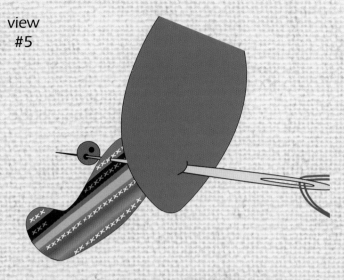

opposite leg, and button as shown in view #6. Stitch back through other side of button and body. Pull thread tight and knot. Pull

view
#6

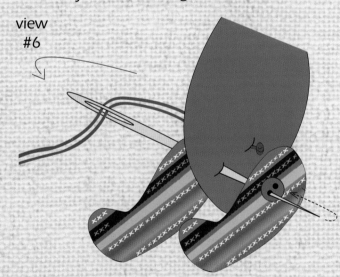

ends back into body. Repeat process to attach arms to bear.

19. Thread beads onto black embroidery thread. Knot around bear's neck. Place ribbon around neck and tie into bow. (Note: Because of small parts, this bear may not be suitable for small children.)

The bear body can be stuffed with a favorite potpourri, or make your own blend, using one of the mixes below.

Potpourri Mixes

Materials for Herbal Garden Potpourri
Crushed bay leaves, dried (½ c.)
Crushed cinnamon sticks, (2)
Globe amaranth, dried (1 c.)
Lemon balm, dried (1 c.)
Lemon verbena, dried (2 c.)
Lemon peel, dried (¼ c.)
Lavender, dried (½ c.)
Lovage root, dried (¼ c.)
Rosemary, dried, (½ c.)
Sage, dried (½ c.)
Thyme, dried (½ c.)
Orris root (2 oz.)
Essential oils: lavender (4 drops), lemon
    verbena (2 drops), rosemary (2 drops)

Materials for Lemon Herb Potpourri
Chamomile flowers, dried (3 c.)
Globe amaranth, dried (1 c.)
Lemon verbena, dried (2 c.)
Rosemary, dried (4 tbsp.)
Orris root (1 oz.)
Essential oils: chamomile (3 drops), lemon
    (6 drops), rosemary oil (2 drops)

General Supplies & Tools
Large mixing bowl
Large reclosable plastic bag

Instructions
1. Mix all materials together in large mixing bowl. Store in plastic bag for six weeks, allowing potpourri scent to mature.

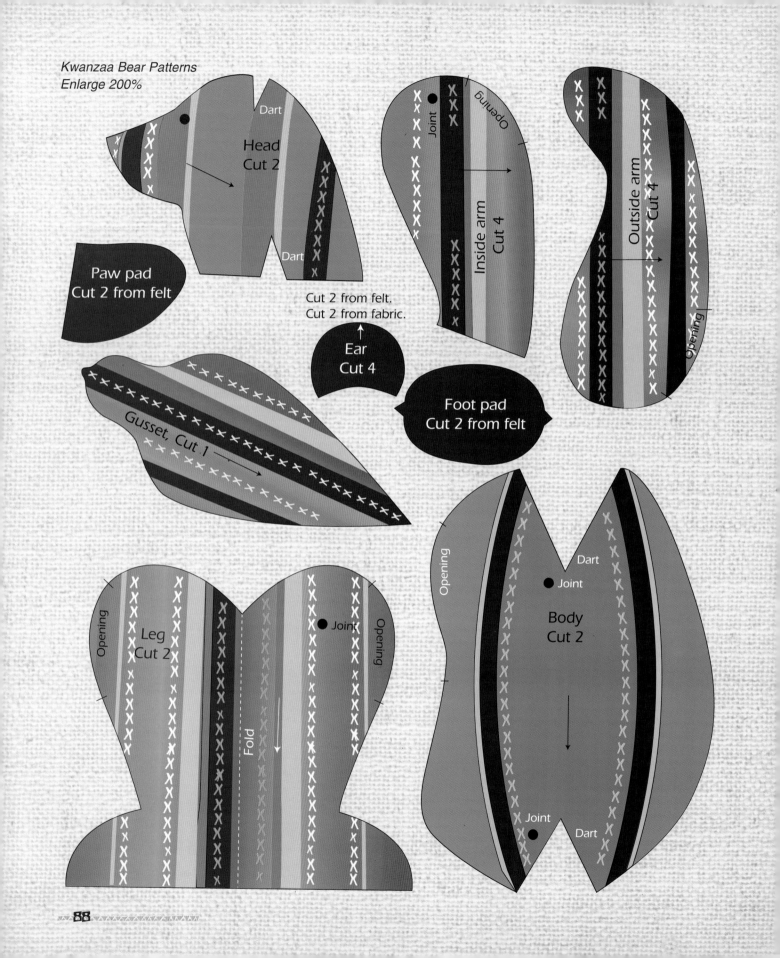

Kwanzaa Bear Patterns
Enlarge 200%

Head
Cut 2

Dart

Dart

Paw pad
Cut 2 from felt

Joint

Opening

Inside arm
Cut 4

Outside arm
Cut 4

Opening

Cut 2 from felt.
Cut 2 from fabric.

Ear
Cut 4

Foot pad
Cut 2 from felt

Gusset, Cut 1

Opening

Body
Cut 2

Dart

Joint

Opening

Leg
Cut 2

Joint

Opening

Fold

Joint

Dart

"Ester, A Tribal Star"
Quilt designed by Tracy Allen
Courtesy of C & T Publishing

Clay Bead Necklace, Rolled-paper Bead Necklace, and Pasta Necklace

Clay Bead Necklace

Materials
Non-toxic, hardening, modeling clay in
    desired colors
Spool of heavyweight thread in
    coordinating color

General Supplies & Tools
Cooking oil
Small kitchen knife
Paper towels
Large safety pin
Cookie sheet

Instructions
1. Knead small amount of clay to soften for molding. Knead each color separately.

2. Hand-roll each color into long strings, approximately 1/16" wide. Align strings and twist them together. Slightly press clay so twists remain in place.

3. Place small amount of cooking oil on paper towel and rub onto knife. Cut clay into desired lengths.

4. Roll each piece of clay in your hands to create circular or oblong beads in desired sizes. Roll one large bead for the center.

view
 #1

5. Rub tip of safety pin with oil and carefully pierce hole in each bead. If clay begins to stick to pin, rub more oil onto pin.

6. Make oblong beads by pushing pin into center of one end of bead. Remove pin and push pin through opposite end of bead.

7. Make circular beads by pushing pin through bead until slightly piercing through opposite side to mark position. Remove pin and push it through tiny marked hole.

8. Arrange beads on cookie sheet and bake, following manufacturer's instructions.

9. Arrange beads in desired order for stringing. Count and align beads before stringing so each type of bead can be evenly spaced on necklace. Begin stringing beads onto thread by tying large bead on one end of thread as shown in view #1. String remaining beads as shown in view #2 until 1" of thread remains. Tie thread ends into knot, then slip loose ends back through center of beads to conceal.

view
 #2

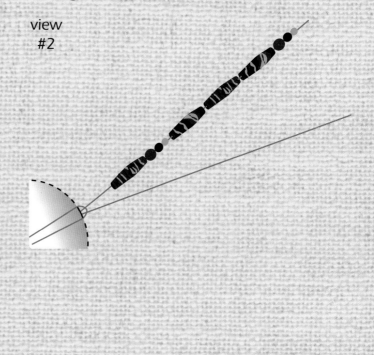

Rolled-paper Bead Necklace

Materials
Magazine clippings
Colored paper
Permanent markers
Elastic thread
Decorative beads (optional)

General Supplies & Tools
Craft scissors
Small crochet hook
Craft glue
Yarn needle

Instructions

1. Select colorful sections from magazine clippings or draw desired designs on paper, using permanent markers.

2. Cut paper into oblong rectangles. Size of rectangles determines width and size of beads.

3. Cut rectangle in half diagonally to form two triangles as shown in view #1.

view #1

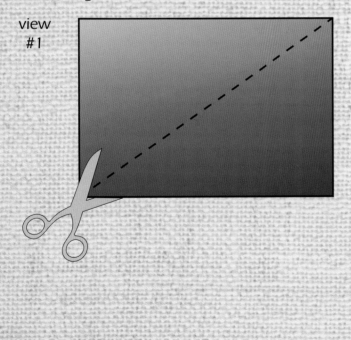

4. Apply craft glue to underside of narrow tip of triangle.

5. Using crochet hook and beginning at wide end of triangle, roll paper to glued tip as shown in view #2. Hold paper onto crochet hook until glued tip is securely stuck to paper. Slip bead off crochet hook. Repeat process until desired number of beads have been made. Allow beads to dry completely before stringing together.

view #2

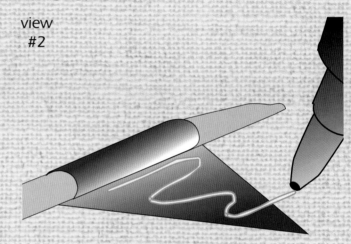

6. Cut elastic thread slightly longer than desired necklace length, then thread elastic onto yarn needle.

7. Tie large knot with 2" tail on one end of elastic to keep beads from slipping off. String decorative beads between paper beads if desired. Tie ends of elastic into knot, then slip loose ends back through center of beads to conceal.

Pasta Necklace

Materials
Assorted uncooked noodles
Food coloring
Elastic thread

General Supplies & Tools
Newspaper
Plastic gloves
Plastic sandwich bags
Craft scissors
Yarn needle

Instructions
1. Cover work area with newspaper, and wear plastic gloves when coloring noodles.

2. Place one handful of noodles in bag, using one bag per color. Sprinkle a few drops of desired food coloring in each bag, blow in some air, twist top closed, then gently shake until noodles are evenly coated. Add more color, if needed. Leave bags open to allow noodles to dry.

3. Cut elastic thread slightly longer than desired length of necklace, then thread elastic onto yarn needle.

4. Tie one noodle to end of elastic thread, leaving a 2" tail, and begin beading. Mix noodle shapes and colors as desired. Untie first noodle, then tie ends of elastic thread into knot. Slip loose ends back through center of noodles to conceal.

Five Cats Necklace and Earrings

Five Cats Necklace and Earrings

Designed by Ann Benson. Project taken from "Beadwork BASICS" courtesy of Sterling Publishing Co., Inc.

Materials

Square clay beads, purchased or handmade:
  ¾" (2), 1" (4), 1⅛" (1)
Leopard skin jasper beads, 8 mm (6)
Metallic gold seed beads: 6/0 (16),
  11/0 (approx. 250)
Gold-finish clasp
Gold-finish crimps (2)
Gold-finish headpins, 1¼" (2)
Gold-finish earwires (2)
Tigertail, 12-lb. test (20")

General Supplies & Tools

Needle-nose pliers
Wire cutters

Instructions
Necklace

1. Thread 6" of 11/0 metallic gold seed beads onto tigertail.

2. Thread one 6/0 metallic gold bead, one leopard skin jasper bead, and one 6/0 metallic gold bead.

3. Thread one ¾" square clay bead and repeat threading order in step 2.

4. Thread one 1" square clay bead and repeat threading order in step 2.

5. Thread 1⅛" square clay bead and repeat threading order in step 2.

6. Repeat threading order in step 4.

7. Repeat threading order in step 3.

8. Repeat threading order in step 1.

9. Slide one crimp over one end of tigertail. Slip end of tigertail through clasp and make loop. Slide free end of tigertail into crimp. Take up slack and using pliers, flatten crimp to secure. Using wire cutters, trim off any excess tigertail. Repeat with other end of tigertail.

Earrings:

1. Thread one 6/0 metallic gold seed bead, one 1" square clay bead, and one 6/0 metallic gold bead onto one headpin. Using wire cutters, trim headpin excess to ¼".

2. Make loop in ¼" end of headpin. Using pliers, close loop around earwire loop.

3. Repeat steps 1 and 2 for second earring.

(Note: Refer page 91 for additional information on handmade clay beads.)

December 31st

Principle: Kuumba or Creativity
To do always as much as we can, in whatever way we can, in order to leave our community more beneficial than we inherited it.
Symbol: Kikombe cha umoja or communal cup
Candle: Red

"Kuumba" is today's answer. The sixth day of Kwanzaa is one of great significance, it is the evening of the Karamu. Six candles are lit this evening. A program that consists of cultural expression in several forms completes the celebrations for this day. Dr. Karenga suggested the following outline for this evening's program:

1. **Kukarihisha** or Welcoming
   Introductory remarks and recognition of distinguished guests and elders
   Cultural expression: songs, music, dance, unity circle, or other expressions

2. **Kukumbuka** or Remembering
   Reflections of a man, a woman, and a child
   Cultural expression

3. **Kuchunguza tena na kutoa ahadi tena** or Reassessment and Recommitment

4. **Kushangilia** or Rejoicing
   Tamshi la tambiko or libation statement
   Kikombe cha umoja or unity cup
   Kutoa majina or calling names of family ancestors and black heroes
   Ngoma or drums
   Karamu or feast
   Cultural expression

5. **Tamshi la tuatonana** or Farewell Statement

Bendera or The Flag of Our People

Red symbolizes the blood that has been shed in our people's long struggles for freedom and fairness.

Black symbolizes the unity of our people under the pressure of separation.

Green symbolizes the future of our people.

Beaded Unity Cup

Beaded Unity Cup

Materials
Large glass goblet
African beads (30" strand)
Beading string (approx. 3 yds.)
Predrilled cowrie shells (7)
Jump rings (7)

General Supplies & Tools
Beading needle
Craft scissors
Needle-nose pliers

Instructions
1. Wash and dry goblet.

2. Using double strand for strength, thread string onto needle about three times longer than diameter of goblet.

3. Thread bead onto string about 4" from end of string, then thread string through bead again to secure to keep other beads from falling off end. Continue to thread beads onto string as desired until strand is long enough to fit around goblet.

4. For scallops, use same method for stringing beads as before. String seven strands of beads 4" long leaving 4" of doubled string at each end of beads, which will allow enough string to tie ends on. Tie each scallop to beaded strand around goblet at 2" intervals.

5. Using needle-nose pliers, bend jump rings and place cowrie shell on ring. Attach one ring and cowrie shell to center of each beaded scallop.

6. Thread beads onto another doubled strand of thread and attach to base of goblet.

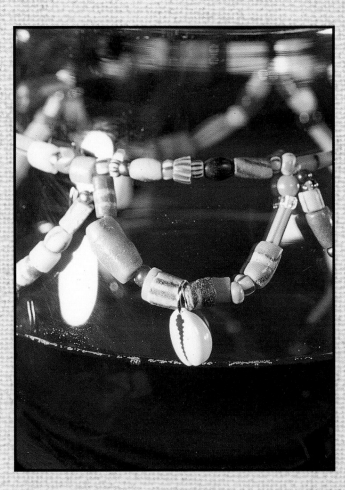

Fruit Punch

16 oz. orange juice
16 oz. pineapple juice
¼ c. lemon juice
2 c. water, cold
6 c. ginger ale
4 tbsp. sugar or honey
20 oz. can fruit cocktail
Ice, cubes or crushed

1. Chill orange and pineapple juices two hours before preparation.

2. Combine all ingredients. Add ice and serve chilled.

Découpage Photo Collage

Découpage Photo Collage

Materials
Assorted photos
Assorted colorful fabric scraps
Matte découpage medium
Birch plywood, ¼" thick in assorted sizes
Black acrylic paint
Matte spray sealer
1" sawtooth picture hanger

General Supplies & Tools
Craft scissors
Paintbrushes: med. flat, sponge
Black fine-tip permanent marker
Scroll saw
Medium-grit sandpaper
Industrial-strength glue

Instructions
1. Make color copies of photos and fabric scraps. If desired, enlarge or reduce photos and fabrics so all are uniform in size.

2. Cut copies of photos into assorted geometric shapes. Cut same shapes from fabric copies about ¾" larger than photos.

3. Refer to General Instructions for Découpage Techniques on pages 122-123. Using flat brush, paint découpage medium on wood. Adhere fabric copies, gently smoothing to release any air bubbles. Allow découpage to dry.

4. Paint découpage medium on fabric copies. Découpage photo copies to center of fabric copies. Apply three coats of découpage over fabric and photo copies, allowing découpage to dry between coats.

5. Using fine-tip marker, draw cutting line ¼" from photo in same shape as photo. Using scroll saw, cut along line.

6. Sand rough edges.

7. Using sponge brush, paint sides and back of wood black. Allow paint to dry.

8. Spray collage with sealer.

9. Arrange and glue photo wood shapes together, layering smaller ones on top corners of larger ones for sturdiness, referring to photo on page 100.

10. Center and glue sawtooth hanger to back of collage.

Painted T-shirts

Painted T-shirts

Materials
T-shirt
Coordinating fabric paints
Colorful fabric (½ yd.)
Double-sided fusible web

General Supplies & Tools
Cardboard or shirt board
Straight pins
Marking pencil
Fabric scissors
Iron/ironing board

Instructions
Painted T-shirt
1. Refer to General Instructions for Fabric Painting Techniques on page 122. Prewash T-shirt. Allow to dry.

2. Slip cardboard inside T-shirt. Pin edges of T-shirt to the cardboard to secure.

3. Using marking pencil, mark desired design on T-shirt.

4. Apply fabric paint over marked lines. Allow paint to dry before removing marking pencil lines. Paint each section separately and allow paint to dry before painting additional sections.

Appliquéd and Painted T-shirt
1. Refer to General Instructions for Fabric Painting Techniques on page 122. Prewash T-shirt. Allow to dry.

2. Design appliqué pattern as desired.

3. Place fusible web, paper side up, on appliqué pattern and trace. Cut fusible web ¼" larger than appliqué pattern.

4. Place fusible web, paper side up, on wrong side of fabric pieces and fuse, following manufacturer's instructions. Trim excess fabric.

5. Cut out appliqué. Remove paper backing and arrange appliqué on T-shirt, then fuse.

6. Slip cardboard inside T-shirt. Pin edges of T-shirt to cardboard to secure.

7. Use marking pencil to draw desired design on T-shirt and appliqué.

8. Apply fabric paint over marked lines. Allow paint to dry before removing the marking pencil lines. Paint each section separately and allow paint to dry before painting additional sections.

Flowerpots

Flowerpots

Materials
Non-toxic, hardening, modeling clay
Clay pots (3)
Acrylic paints: dk. green, lt. green, dk. red,
    lt. red.
Crackle medium
Spray sealer

General Supplies & Tools
Jewelry or buttons with raised Afrocentric
    patterns (3)
Craft glue
Paintbrush

Instructions
1. Roll three 1" pieces of modeling clay into balls. Flatten balls into ¼"-thick ovals. Gently press jewelry or button into center of one clay oval and remove. Using remaining jewelry or buttons, repeat above process on remaining clay ovals. Bake clay, according to manufacturer's instructions. Glue clay oval to front of each pot.

2. Paint inside and outside of one pot dk. green. Paint remaining pots dk. red. Allow paint to dry. Paint a liberal amount of crackle medium over inside and outside of pots, following manufacturer's instructions. Paint lt. green paint over dk. green pot. Allow paint to dry. Repeat process on dk. red pots with lt. red paint.

3. Spray inside and outside of each pot with sealer.

Traditional African dishes can be served along with family favorites for the Karamu. Try Curry Chicken, below, served with Roti on page 106.

Curry Chicken

2 tbsp. curry powder
1 tbsp. cumin
1 tsp. cinnamon
1 tsp. garlic powder
Med. onion, chopped
2 tbsp. vegetable oil
2 lbs. boneless chicken, cubed
Water
2 chicken boullion cubes
2 med. potatoes, peeled, quartered

1. Mix curry powder, cumin, cinnamon, garlic, onion, and oil together.

2. Stir chicken into spice mixture and coat completely.

3. Place coated chicken in cooking pot and cover with water. Add boullion cubes to water.

4. Simmer over low heat, stirring frequently to prevent meat from sticking to bottom of pan.

5. When meat is almost cooked, add potatoes and continue to simmer, stirring occasionally until potatoes and chicken are completely cooked.

6. Serve with Roti or flatbread.

Roti (or Chapatis)

2½ c. all-purpose flour
½ tsp. salt
2 tsp. baking soda
1 c. water
4 tbsp. vegetable oil, divided

1. Mix flour, salt, and baking soda together.

2. Mix water into dry ingredients forming a stiff dough.

3. Using rolling pin, roll out dough into a circle. Brush 1 tbsp. oil onto dough.

4. Fold dough in half and pinch dough together.

5. Flour surface, roll dough out again, and brush with 1 tbsp. oil. Fold dough in half and pinch together. Repeat this process two more times.

6. Set dough aside for ½ hour to rest.

7. Divide dough into six equal pieces and roll into balls.

8. Flour surface and roll out each ball into thin circle.

9. Oil griddle and heat until hot. Place one roti onto hot griddle. When roti begins to puff up, brush oil on topside of dough.

10. Continue to bake on griddle until light brown spots appear on underside of roti.

11. Turn roti over, brush oil on topside, and grill roti until light brown spots appear on underside. Repeat with remaining roti.

12. Remove cooked roti from grill and allow to cool enough to be held in hands. Clap cooked roti between the palms of your hands to increase flakiness. Repeat with remaining roti.

13. Fold roti into thirds and serve with Curry Chicken.

"African Tapestry"
Quilt designed by Christine Davis
Courtesy of C & T Publishing

January 1st

Principle: Imani or Faith
To believe with all our heart in our people, our parents, our teachers, our leaders, and in the righteousness and victory of our struggle.
Symbol: Mishumaa saba or the seven candles of Kwanzaa
Candle: Green

   The day begins with the question "Habari gani?" and is answered with "Imani." The last candle is lit and a libation ceremony is performed for the last time in this Kwanzaa holiday. This is the beginning of the New Year and a time to look to the future.

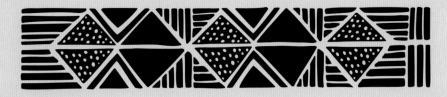

Imani
by Marcia O. McNair

For African Americans, Kwanzaa is a holiday—
It's a time when our families come together in a special way
To learn about the past, present, and future dreams
Of our many great and beautiful African Americans.

The kings and queens of the great African kingdoms,
Our leaders of the past and today, who encouraged us to freedom.
The talents of our artists and of our fine musicians,
Our teachers and our preachers, who teach positive lessons.
Our doctors, lawyers, and scientists, who continue to share
     their knowledgeable gifts,
And most of all. . .to be proud of our accomplishments.

Yes,
For African Americans, Kwanzaa is a holiday,
It's a time when our families come together in a special way
To learn about the past, present, and future dreams
Of our many great and beautiful African Americans.

Oxtail Switch

Oxtail Switch

Materials
Decorative ribbon, 1½"-wide (1½ yds.), or
   6" x 13" piece of colorful fabric
Empty paper towel roll
Scrap of brown material (leather, felt,
   or cloth)
Assorted beads
Small bells
Beading wire (14")
Cording in three assorted colorful shades
   (14" each)
Unspun wool fleece (24")

General Supplies & Tools
Hot-glue gun and glue sticks
Fabric scissors

Instructions
1. Wrap and hot-glue decorative ribbon or fabric around paper towel roll, tucking and gluing ends to inside of roll.

2. Cut brown material into a 3" x 6" rectangle. Wrap and glue material around top of roll, making certain 2" of material sticks up over the top of the roll. Leave end open.

3. String beads and bells onto beading wire as desired. Braid cording. Twist strung wire and cording together to form a handle. Knot ends.

4. Hot-glue handle ends to top inside of roll. Fold material across top, slitting as necessary around handle ends, then glue closed. Hot-glue beads and bells on top of material.

5. Fold wool in half. Lightly comb with fingers to smooth together. Hot-glue folded end into bottom of roll.

It is considered "good luck" by some to have black-eyed peas and rice on New Year's Day. Try this family favorite and bring "good luck" to your New Year.

Rice and Black-eyed Peas

5 strips of bacon
Med. onion, sliced
½ c. sugar
12 oz. can black-eyed peas
1½ c. instant rice
8 oz. can tomato sauce
1 c. water

1. Fry bacon in four qt. Dutch oven until crisp. Remove bacon, leaving drippings in Dutch oven.

2. Brown onion in Dutch oven and remove.

3. Brown ½ cup sugar in Dutch oven.

4. Pour black-eyed peas with liquid to sugar in Dutch oven and mix.

5. Add rice, tomato sauce, and water to Dutch oven. Bring to boil, stirring occasionally. Simmer until rice is cooked. Bacon and onions can also be returned to Dutch oven at this time, or mixed in after rice is cooked.

Decorative Transfer Pillow

Decorative Transfer Pillow

Materials
Fabric: bleached muslin (10" x 11½"), African
  motif cotton (½ yd.)
Pillow form (16")
Fabric transfer medium
Coordinating ribbon: 1½" (1¼ yd.)

General Supplies and Tools
Flat paintbrush
Rolling pin
Clean rag
Sponge
Sewing machine
Coordinating thread
Fabric glue
Fabric scissors

Instructions
1. Enlarge zebra artwork 130% and color copy.

2. Paint fabric transfer medium onto color copy, following manufacturer's instructions. Turn copy with medium side down and place on center of bleached muslin fabric. Using a rolling pin, smooth copy out. Using wet rag, clean excess medium off . Allow medium to dry 24-48 hours.

3. Using wet sponge, rub paper off of transfer. (Note: It may require sponging several times to remove the paper.) Allow fabric to dry.

4. Using glue, adhere ribbon around artwork to frame, mitering corners.

5. Cut two 3¾" x 17" strips, two 3" x 10" strips, and one 17" x 17" square from African motif fabrics.

6. Machine-stitch 3" x 10" strips with ¼" seams to 10" sides of muslin fabric. Machine-stitch 3¾" x 17" strips with ¼" seams to top and bottom of muslin and 3" x 10" strips. This forms front of pillow. Place right side of pillow front to right side of 17" x 17" fabric, machine-stitch ¼" seam around edges, leaving a 10" opening to insert pillow form. Insert pillow form and stitch opening closed.

Kente Cloth Laminated Bag

Kente Cloth Laminated Bag

Materials
Colorful cotton African motif fabric (3 yds.)
Iron-on vinyl (2 yds.)

General Supplies & Tools
Fabric scissors
Iron/ironing board
Sewing machine
Black thread
Masking tape

Instructions

1. Cut a 30" x 20" fabric panel for bag, two 14" x 12" panels for sides of bag, and two 22" x 2" strips for handles.

2. Measure and cut vinyl 1" larger than all fabric pieces. Before bonding, test vinyl on scrap fabric.

3. Center and press vinyl to right side of fabric, following manufacturer's instructions, one piece at a time.

4. Trim vinyl from sides and bottom of side panels and from sides of bag, but leave the excess vinyl at top edges. Fold excess vinyl over to back of fabric and bond as before.

5. Snip off small triangles from corners of handles, then fold excess vinyl to back of fabric and bond.

6. With right sides together and a ¼" seam, machine-stitch side panels to bag. Machine-

stitch squared edges of panels to give bag a defined shape as shown in view #1.

view #1

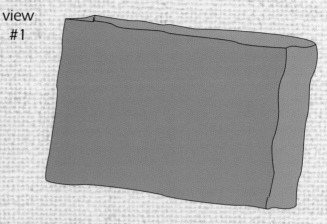

7. Trim seams to ⅛". Turn bag right side out and finger-press seams open. Machine-stitch ¼" encasing seam, with previous seam inside, around each side panel as shown in view #2.

view #2

8. Fold top edge of bag inward ¼" and machine-stitch to hem as shown in view #3.

view #3

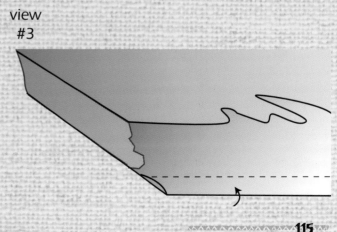

9. Fold the handles in half width-wise and machine-stitch a narrow seam along edges as shown in view 4.

view #4

10. Center 2" of one handle end on bag and temporarily hold in place with tape. Machine-stitch ends to bag as shown in view #5. Reinforce handles by sewing over first stitches several times. Repeat process for remaining handle.

view #5

Harvest Pin Cushion

Materials
Terra cotta flowerpot, 3"
African motif fabric, 5½" circle
Polyester stuffing
Corsage pins (3 or more)
Sculpting clay
Acrylic paints
Spray sealer

General Supplies & Tools
Sewing needle
Coordinating thread
Glue: craft, super
Wire cutters
Paintbrushes

Instructions
1. Using needle and thread, sew a gathering stitch around fabric circle. Pull strings slightly to gather, and stuff firmly with polyester stuffing. Pull strings tighter and check for fit inside upper edge of flowerpot.

2. Using craft glue, glue stuffed fabric, gathered edges down, into flowerpot.

3. Shape sculpting clay into fruit or vegetable shapes. Using wire cutters, cut heads from corsage pins. Push top of pin into bottom of fruit and vegetable shapes ¼". Remove pins and bake fruits and vegetables, following manufacturer's instructions.

4. Using super glue, glue pins into fruits and vegetables. Paint fruits and vegetables as desired. Spray with clear sealer and embellish pins as desired. Place in pincushion.

Karamu Apron

Karamu Apron

Materials
Apron
Colorful fabric (½ yd.)
Double-sided fusible web
Coordinating fabric paints

General Supplies & Tools
Fabric scissors
Iron/ironing board
Straight pins
Cardboard or shirt board
Marking pencil

Instructions
1. Refer to General Instructions for Fabric Painting Techniques on page 122. Wash apron and fabric. Allow to dry.

2. Design appliqué patterns as desired.

3. Place fusible web, paper side up, on appliqué patterns and trace. Cut fusible web ¼" larger than appliqué patterns.

4. Place fusible web, paper side up, on wrong side of fabric pieces and fuse, following manufacturer's instructions. Trim excess fabric.

5. Cut out appliqués. Remove paper backing and arrange appliqués on apron, then fuse in place.

6. Place cardboard under apron. Pin apron to cardboard to secure.

7. Using marking pencil, draw desired design on apron and appliqués.

8. Apply fabric paint over marked lines. Allow paint to dry before removing marking pencil lines. Paint each section separately and allow paint to dry before painting additional sections.

Aunt Idalia's Pancakes

1 egg
1 tsp. vanilla extract
¾ c. sugar, divided
2 c. water
1 c. all-purpose flour
¾ c. raisins
2 tsp. oil

1. Beat egg in large bowl until frothy. Stir vanilla extract and ½ cup sugar into egg.

2. Stir water into mixture. Sift flour into mixture and beat. Stir raisins into batter.

3. Place 2 tsp. oil into 8" skillet and heat over medium heat. Pour ¼ cup batter into heated skillet and spread out to sides of pan.

4. Turn pancake over when light brown and cook other side until light brown.

5. Place ¼ cup sugar onto plate. Remove pancake, fold into thirds, and roll in sugar. Serve immediately.

6. Repeat until all batter is used.

Decorative Edge Scarf and African Scarf

African Scarf

Materials
Colorful African motif cotton fabric (1-2 yds.)
Coordinating thread

General Supplies & Tools
Fabric scissors
Sewing machine

Instructions
1. Cut fabric into desired size: 6" x 42" for men and children; 36" square, 60" square, or 60" x 70" rectangle for women.

2. Roll and sew ¼" hem around all edges, or fray narrow ends of fabric, then hem sides only.

Fabric selection for scarves—
◆ Select fabric for a scarf that is drapable. Soft, silky fabrics drape well and tie easily.

Variations:
1. Blanket stitch edges of hemmed scarf, using size 20 chenille needle and coordinating pearl cotton.

2. Crochet ends of scarf, using mercerized crochet cotton.

3. Sew commercially manufactured fringe to ends of scarf.

4. Bead edges of scarf, using beading needle and fine silk thread or cotton embroidery floss.

Decorative Edge Scarf

Materials:
Fabric: 60" wide (⅞ yd.), scraps coordinating colors for balled edges (3)
Polyester fiber fill
Pearl cotton, coordinating color
Fringe: knotted 4" (2 yds.), brush 1" (½ yd.)
Fray preventative
Braid (2¾ yds.)
Satin cording (6 yds.)
Beads: pony (96), metal (72)

General Supplies & Tools
Fabric scissors
Coordinating thread
Sewing machine
Iron/ironing board
Needles: sewing, tapestry size #18

Instructions:
1. Cut two 14½" x 60" pieces from 60" fabric. With right sides together, machine-stitch two pieces together, taking ¼" seam, leaving short ends open. Turn right side out.

2. Cut twenty-four 1" x 2½" pieces from each fabric scrap color for balled edges. With right sides together, machine-stitch two long edges and one short edge, taking ¼" seams to form tube.

3. Stuff open end of tube with polyester fiber fill. Wrap open end tightly with pearl cotton as shown in view #1.

view #1

4. Using iron, press ¼" seam under on short ends of scarf. Using sewing needle and thread, stitch eighteen balled edges, evenly spaced between ironed edges, onto one short end of scarf. Using sewing

machine, topstitch scarf ends and balled edges together. Repeat on other scarf end.

5. Measure and cut knotted fringe into four 14" lengths. Apply fray preventative liberally at cut marks. Let fray preventative dry. Using sewing needle and thread, stitch one length each to bottom front and bottom back of scarf fabric. Repeat on other scarf end.

6. Measure and cut braid into four 14" lengths. Apply fray preventative liberally at cut marks. Let fray preventative dry. Trim braid, if needed. Stitch one length of braid on top of knotted fringe edge on front. Stitch second length of braid 2" above first braid. Repeat on other scarf end.

7. Measure and cut cording into two 48" lengths. Apply fray preventative. Pinch and twist ends until fray preventative dries or holds form. Working with one length, fold one end 2" back on itself and tie a topknot as shown in view #2.

view #2

8. Cut off short tail and apply fray preventative. String five pony beads onto long length of cording. Tie knot tightly at bottom of last bead. (Note: Do not cut loop from long end until beads are strung and knotted.) Cut off tail and apply fray preventative. Repeat process until twelve beaded cords are completed.

9. Apply fray preventative to tops of twelve knotted brush tassels. When completely dry, cut knotted tassels from braid top, flush with knot. Stitch one knotted tassel to bottom knot of each beaded tassel.

10. Evenly space six beaded tassels along bottom front edge of scarf. Stitch corded knot on top of braid. Repeat on other scarf end.

11. Cut eighteen 1" pieces of brush fringe. Apply fray preventative liberally at cut marks. Let fray preventative dry. Set aside.

12. Measure and cut cording into two 56" lengths. Apply fray preventative. Pinch and twist ends until fray preventative dries or holds form. Working with one length, fold one end 2" back on itself and tie a topknot as shown in view #2. String one metal bead, two pony beads, and one metal bead onto cording.

13. Using one 1" length of brush fringe and sewing needle and thread, tack left edge to cording. Roll fringe piece around cording and tack closed. Using tapestry needle with six strands of pearl cotton, bring pearl cotton up through bottom of tassel. Wrap pearl cotton twice around base of tassel head, through head body, then wrap top part of tassel head twice as shown in view #3. Knot pearl cotton and run tail back through body. Push fringe back and clip both pearl cotton and cording as shown in view #4. Repeat for all tassels.

view #3

view #4

14. Evenly space nine tassels on each end of scarf along top length of braid. Stitch into place.

General Instructions

Fabric Painting Techniques

Prewash all fabric to be used. Fabric should be ironed and stretched flat.

Place cardboard behind fabric to keep paint from bleeding through onto work surface. Secure with pins to hold in place.

Paint can be applied straight from bottle to form outlines or painted directly on fabric with paintbrush. Allow paint to dry.

Follow paint manufacturer's instructions for washing and cleaning fabric that has been painted.

Découpage Techniques

Using a large flat brush, brush a liberal coat of découpage medium onto surface.

Place paper cutout over wet découpage medium and, using fingers,
gently smooth out air bubbles or folds.

A brayer or wooden dowel may also be used for smoothing. Allow découpage
medium to dry. Apply two additional coats of découpage medium
over image, allowing medium to dry between coats.

Rubber Stamping Techniques

Ink Application

Ink can be applied to rubber stamps by using an ink pad or rubber stamp markers.

Rubber stamp markers allow multiple colors along with more color detail. When using a marker on rubber stamps, the color may dry before stamping. Misting the stamp, using a fine mist spray bottle filled with water, will remoisten the ink. Or, simply exhale on the stamp to remoisten.

Embossing

Use an embossing or slow drying pigment ink pad, heat-sensitive embossing powder, and an embossing heat tool. A light bulb or toaster will also work, but do not use a hair dryer.

For one-color embossing, stamp the image, using embossing ink.

Pour embossing powder on stamped image and tap off excess.

Using heat tool, apply heat until embossing powder melts.

Acknowledgements

Marcia Odle McNair is an artist and educator residing in the New York area. She is a college level Fine Arts instructor, leads workshops on the Arts for educators, and teaches grade school children.

Marcia was inspired to share craft ideas that can be made as gifts or decorations, as well as created in group activities during the celebration of Kwanzaa.

From the Author

I would like to acknowledge the following special individuals for their contributions and encouragement in making this book possible:

Special thanks to my husband Keith McNair for contributing original poems and stories and who continues to be supportive throughout my many creative endeavors.

To my mother, Sheila Nedd Odle for her expertise in sewing and craft techniques, as well as her knowledge of family traditions.

To my father, Oswald Pelham Odle for encouraging me to pursue my dreams.

To my dear friend, Juanita James, who took my idea seriously and steered me in the right direction.

In addition, I would like to thank the following family and friends for sharing recipes, suggestions, advice, and support: Myrna Ortiz: Avril, Andrea, and Andrew Campbell; Carol Cruckshank; Sandra Holmes; Laura Carrington, Grace Braithwaite; Eustace and Barbara Nedd; Coseta Odle; Mark Odle; Anthony Barboza; Michele Godwin; and Loria Tucker.

We would like to offer our sincere appreciation to Roberta Horton, author of "The Fabric Makes the Quilt," and the following artists for photographs and reprint permission on: "African Critters" by Susan Maynard Arnold, "African Tapestry" by Christine Davis, "Ester, A Tribal Star" by Tracy Allen, and "Jambo Africa" by Joan Helm.

Quilts photo credit: Sharon Risedorph of San Francisco, CA.

Portrait photo credits: Quick's Photo of Westbury, NY and LifeTouch National School Studios, Inc. of Oceanside, NY.

"Five Cats Necklace and Earrings" was designed by Ann Benson. Project taken from "Beadwork BASICS" courtesy of Sterling Publishing Co., Inc.

DMC Corporation
10 Port Kearney Bldg.
South Kearney, NJ 07032-4688

Deco Arts
Americana Paints
P.O. Box 386
Stanford, KY 40484

Delta Technical Coatings
2550 Pellissier Place
Whittier, CA 90601
*Available through arts and crafts stores nationwide

Plaid Enterprises, Inc.
P.O. Box 7600
Norcross, GA 30091-7600
Tel. 1-800-842-4197

Woodland Sales
Quick Grab, Inc.
P.O. Box 15040
Scottsdale, AZ 85267-5040
Tel. 1-602-473-0005

Zweigart
2 Riverview Dr.
Somerset, NJ 08873
For information e-mail: Zweigart.com

Metric Equivalency Chart

mm-millimetres   cm-centimetres
inches to millimetres and centimetres

inches	mm	cm	inches	cm	inches	cm
⅛	3	0.3	9	22.9	30	76.2
¼	6	0.6	10	25.4	31	78.7
½	13	1.3	12	30.5	33	83.8
⅝	16	1.6	13	33.0	34	86.4
¾	19	1.9	14	35.6	35	88.9
⅞	22	2.2	15	38.1	36	91.4
1	25	2.5	16	40.6	37	94.0
1¼	32	3.2	17	43.2	38	96.5
1½	38	3.8	18	45.7	39	99.1
1¾	44	4.4	19	48.3	40	101.6
2	51	5.1	20	50.8	41	104.1
2½	64	6.4	21	53.3	42	106.7
3	76	7.6	22	55.9	43	109.2
3½	89	8.9	23	58.4	44	111.8
4	102	10.2	24	61.0	45	114.3
4½	114	11.4	25	63.5	46	116.8
5	127	12.7	26	66.0	47	119.4
6	152	15.2	27	68.6	48	121.9
7	178	17.8	28	71.1	49	124.5
8	203	20.3	29	73.7	50	127.0

yards to metres

yards	metres	yards	metres	yards	metres	yards	metres	yards	metres
⅛	0.11	2⅛	1.94	4⅛	3.77	6⅛	5.60	8⅛	7.43
¼	0.23	2¼	2.06	4¼	3.89	6¼	5.72	8¼	7.54
⅜	0.34	2⅜	2.17	4⅜	4.00	6⅜	5.83	8⅜	7.66
½	0.46	2½	2.29	4½	4.11	6½	5.94	8½	7.77
⅝	0.57	2⅝	2.40	4⅝	4.23	6⅝	6.06	8⅝	7.89
¾	0.69	2¾	2.51	4¾	4.34	6¾	6.17	8¾	8.00
⅞	0.80	2⅞	2.63	4⅞	4.46	6⅞	6.29	8⅞	8.12
1	0.91	3	2.74	5	4.57	7	6.40	9	8.23
1⅛	1.03	3⅛	2.86	5⅛	4.69	7⅛	6.52	9⅛	8.34
1¼	1.14	3¼	2.97	5¼	4.80	7¼	6.63	9¼	8.46
1⅜	1.26	3⅜	3.09	5⅜	4.91	7⅜	6.74	9⅜	8.57
1½	1.37	3½	3.20	5½	5.03	7½	6.86	9½	8.69
1⅝	1.49	3⅝	3.31	5⅝	5.14	7⅝	6.97	9⅝	8.80
1¾	1.60	3¾	3.43	5¾	5.26	7¾	7.09	9¾	8.92
1⅞	1.71	3⅞	3.54	5⅞	5.37	7⅞	7.20	9⅞	9.03
2	1.83	4	3.66	6	5.49	8	7.32	10	9.14

Index